A VIEW
FROM THE ALLEY

by Aubrey S. Darby

with an introduction by Judy Darby

TO MY CHILDREN

Published August 2012
by Judith Darby

First published in 1974 by Luton Museum

© Judith Darby, 2012 and Aubrey Darby, 1974.

The right of Judith Darby and Aubrey Darby to be identified as the authors of this work has been assumed by them in accordance with the Copyright, Designs and Patents Act 1988

ISBN 978 1 898841 28 9

Designed and typeset by Tracey Moren,
Moren Associates Limited, www.morenassociates.co.uk

Printed in Great Britain by TJ International, Padstow, Cornwall

Front cover picture: Fifteen-year-old Aubrey Darby, with his nephew, proudly showing off his new bicycle. Mary Ann Darby is in the background. (Circa 1920)

Contents

Acknowledgements

First and foremost I owe a debt of gratitude to Luton Museum for their permission for this book to be re-printed. From Dr. Elizabeth Adey I have received unfailing courtesy and assistance, and also from Chris Grabham. Their kindness, help and professionalism is greatly appreciated, as is their permission to use the photographs from the original book.

Pamela Birch, at Bedfordshire Archives, patiently gave me advice and help in locating photographs of Dunstable Road, the Town Hall before and after the fire, the Corn Exchange, and a Diamond Foundry receipt card. I would like to thank Bedfordshire Archives for permission to use these photographs.

Two departments at The Victoria and Albert Museum, Photographs and Textiles, advised on the date of the cover photograph, and I would like to thank them for their courtesy and expertise. Jayne Shrimpton also gave expert advice on a precise dating, for which I am very grateful.

Once again *The Book Castle* has proved invaluable in agreeing to help me publish yet another book, and I would like to thank Paul Bowes and Sally Siddons for all their help, guidance and meticulous attention to detail.

As always I am indebted to my wise friend, Val Goodyear, who was always on hand to advise and help with research.

Judy Darby April 2012

Introduction

Over the years I have had many requests for a copy of *A View from the Alley*, which was published in 1974, two years after my father's death. But I have had to disappoint: it has long since been out of print. I now feel that it is time it was resurrected, along with the vivid characters of my father's boyhood. The book travelled far, and my American niece came across a copy in Missouri University. Then there were the requests from students to be allowed to quote from the book.

Three years before he died, my father took me on a walk round Luton, pointing out to me the landmarks he had known so well as a child, and, as we approached Christ Church School in Buxton Road, we saw it was in the process of being demolished. Hurrying up to the foreman, my father asked if they had found the essays in the school museum.

'No, mate,' said the foreman, puzzled. 'The place was emptied of everything before we came on site.'

'Oh,' said my father, 'I had an essay in that museum. I was good at composition and they put exceptional work on show, there.'

He turned away disappointed, and I reminded him as gently as possible that he was talking of nearly sixty years ago, and that the museum and his work were probably long gone.

'I know,' he said. 'You'll understand one day. To me, it's yesterday.'

A few years later he made a last, nostalgic walk alone, round the town he loved. He knew that he had not long to live, but kept that knowledge to himself, not even consulting a doctor.

In the final chapter of this book he recounts that journey, expressing both sorrow and anger at what he saw:

Stuart Street, what have they done? Destruction, desecration and desolation; is nothing sacrosanct in furthering the progress of the horseless carriage?

There is a terrible poignancy in his musings and imaginings as he makes his way round the town:

I go back, to walk the streets of my childhood, to relieve the ache inside me...perchance I may see some childhood mate, someone who has survived the years.

He reasons that most are long since gone, *yet in the shades of eternity they may be peering out.*

His walk raises the spectres of those he remembers with such clarity, originally seen through the unambiguity and innocence of childhood eyes. At the end of his walk he reflects again on the car and the bulldozer, which are ripping his beloved landscape apart:

The one will strangle with its noxious breath, the other will mangle, no stopping for breath. So be it, my days are numbered, I shall escape the living death.

Inevitably, the day has come when I, too, see the distant past as merely yesterday. I, too, walk round Luton and Dunstable, and search faces for people I once knew, expecting to find them unchanged.

A few weeks ago I retraced my father's last walk round the town, with my oldest friend, and skilled genealogist, Val Goodyear. She was a fitting companion for several reasons, among them that she knew my father well and that he played football with her uncle as a youngster. While he was writing this book he sometimes read extracts aloud to her, for her opinion.

We met on a damp, miserable day outside the Town Hall, by the war memorial recording the names of those who gave their lives in the Great War. I was early, and as I waited, I gazed upwards through the meandering raindrops to read the name of Frederick George Darby, my uncle, who went down with his ship at the age of sixteen. There is no mention of that in *A View from the Alley*, nor of his mother's grief. There is also no mention of the two half sisters who died in 1914 and 1918, one from nephritis, and the other a victim of the terrible influenza epidemic of 1918. Mary Ann Darby lost three children in six years, but she never lost her indomitable spirit.

We began our walk outside the house where my father spent his earliest years, Ivy Road, leading down to Luton Town football ground. Curiously, my father makes no mention of this house, yet he moved here soon after his birth at Coupees Place, Castle Street, and spent his first six years here. Nor, although he was a football lover, did he comment on the close proximity of the ground from where he would have heard the roars of the crowd every home match.

The houses are terraced and substantial enough, with a front parlour, back room, scullery and three bedrooms. The lavatory would have been in the small back yard. I stood outside and imagined a small, scruffy boy come hurling out of the front door, racing down the road to join his pals, intent on mischief. He would try not to think about the father who had left home, but would be all too aware of that fact when his mother dressed him in rags to look, if that was possible, even more poverty-stricken.

He would then be sent round to the house where his father lived with his latest woman, to ask for money. My father responded to this humiliation thirty years later, for when Walter was down on his luck and came looking for his son, he threw him out of the house.

Shortly afterwards the family moved to 16 Grove Road, a few roads away, to the home of another Mary Ann Darby, Walter's aunt by marriage, a well-off widow of a butcher. Perhaps she offered them a refuge because she disapproved of her philandering nephew. The house no longer stands, but the 1911 Census shows that it was no bigger than the one in Ivy Road, and the fresh intake would have had the house bursting at the seams.

But my grandmother did not abuse her kind aunt's hospitality, for she rapidly moved on to Adelaide Street. We followed the route taken by Mary Ann and her children up and down the steep inclines in the area. They would have found another back street, another alley, and a two-up, two-down, with a backyard, all demolished long since. This was the house where my father could see Clarke's butcher shop through the front window, where he worked part time from the age of eight.

We turned the corner into Buxton Road, where Diddle Smith, his childhood friend lived, opposite Christ Church School, which my father and I had watched being demolished. That was the day he asked about his essay in the museum. Diddle's house is gone, too, and a police station was put on the school site. My father would probably say that one punitive regime had been replaced by another.

Finally, the family settled at 7 Princess Street, only a fraction of what it had been, as most of its members were now dispersed or dead. Until 1921, my father's older sister Hettie was part of the household, then she married and moved to Dunstable, and Mary Ann and my father, her youngest son, lived together in harmony. While living here, he and Diddle acquired a puppy.

It died from distemper. *What religion we had, died with its passing.* When he went to convalesce at Biscot after having peritonitis, he stayed in a cottage a few hundred yards from the churchyard where he now lies. Not long before he died he stood outside the church, which then adjoined a school, reflecting:

> *Had anyone pondered what they had in mind, the ancients who plotted playground and graveyard side by side?*

It was from the house in Princess Street that he would walk with his mother to visit her friends in the workhouse, and absorb her strong feelings about the appalling way the old were treated by society. He writes: *The old people didn't last long once inside, not so much heart failure as broken heart.* From her tears and anger on the way home from each of these visits, grew his first stirrings of the socialism which he embraced all his life.

Val Goodyear has often commented that my father is a genealogist's nightmare, as in this book he offers no help or clues at all about his family history. His mother comes and goes through the pages, a powerful, loving force in his life, greatly respected. *Ma's word was law.* We never meet his father: *I never got to know Pa, he hopped it before I was old enough to recognise him.* In fact the 1911 Census shows Walter Darby was still around when my father was five, but a stranger to his son. I suppose being sent to beg money from him could not be construed as a relationship, and my father chooses not to mention that in this book.

The only other mention made of Walter is when my father writes of the aftermath of The Great War, with disillusioned soldiers looting and setting fire to the Town Hall. Bewildered, he comments to his mother that Walter hadn't set fire to buildings when he came home from the Boer War. *'Him? Set light to anything? He was too idle to light the kitchen stove.'*

Anyone reading this book could be forgiven for thinking that the Darby household consisted of just mother and son, but there are clues as to others living with them. My father comments on the *musty odour of rising dampness and overcrowded habitation.* In 1911, the Census records one of his married half sisters and her husband living in the small house in Ivy Road. In addition there was another half sister, Walter was still around, and all four children from the second marriage crowded the rooms.

My father was equally unforthcoming about his family in conversation, although I did piece some facts together, discovering that there had been a family rift, particularly virulent between him and his sister Hettie.

However, in January 1971, he wrote a letter to my eldest sister, stating that his nephew had recently visited him and invited him to his half sister's funeral. Even in that letter he offers no names, and I had to go searching through back copies of *The Luton News*, in the obituaries, to find that this was Gertrude Elizabeth, his mother's eldest daughter by her first marriage.

He wrote:

I thought she had passed on twenty years ago, but she had lived until eighty-five. I, being the last surviving member of the family, was asked to attend her funeral...

He went to the funeral and found numerous nephews and nieces, all anxious to become acquainted.

I left them, my kinsfolk, proud that they should seek me out, and thankful that the old vendettas of my boyhood have all passed away.

Dr. Dony commented in the first edition of this book, that my father was *a keen observer, leaving the reader constantly wondering how different his story would have been if the circumstances of his life had been changed.*

I echo that thought, and remember the years that my father planned this book. He longed to write, had so little time with a gruelling job as foundry foreman at Bagshawe Conveyors, in Dunstable, a sick wife and a large brood of children.

He would tell us the stories that he later set down in this book, and we never tired of hearing about Brother Duck, chorusing, *Quack, quack, quack,* at the appropriate moment in the tale.

Indeed, Aubrey Darby was a frustrated intellectual, one who was well aware that education was out of the reach of his social class. He writes of Diddle's wonderful singing voice, saying, *like so many of our class and generation, his talent was allowed to decay.*

My father's outlet was his reading and writing, and debating politics with his friends. I remember the rolls of paper he brought home from work to write on. In a household where money for the meter ran out on Tuesday, he couldn't afford to buy any. It wasn't until most of us had left home, and he found himself a widower, that he was finally able to indulge his dream of finishing his book. Even then he barely completed it before his death. And if my brother, Tony, had not paid for it to be privately printed and circulated, it might never have seen the light of day.

Remembering that Dr. Dony had visited my father a few months before he died, and given him great encouragement, Tony sent him a copy. The rest is history.

৵৹৻

If my father were alive today he would find that the roads still weave their way through the town, still fiercely hold on to the memories of a bygone age. If I listen hard enough, can I hear the horses' steady trot and the cries of children kicking a ball round streets which hold no terror of cars? Can I hear the school bell toll for pupils long gone, many to early graves because of war and pestilence? If I stand in silence, can I catch the whisper of women on their doorsteps, ripping apart some other's reputation?

In my daydream my father appears round the corner, scruffy, defiant, a determined look on his young face, and I realise he will grow up to inhabit a world full of different hardship, more subtle, more threatening. And I remember his preface to this book:

If comparison be not too odious, the educated society of today has spewed up an intellectual society, obsessed with a need for stimulation...psychoanalysis...delving back to the mother's womb, the parents getting the blame. Could it be that our environment of ignorance made for a more contented and stable society?

I never had the chance to debate that point with him. A few weeks later he died.

Judy Darby

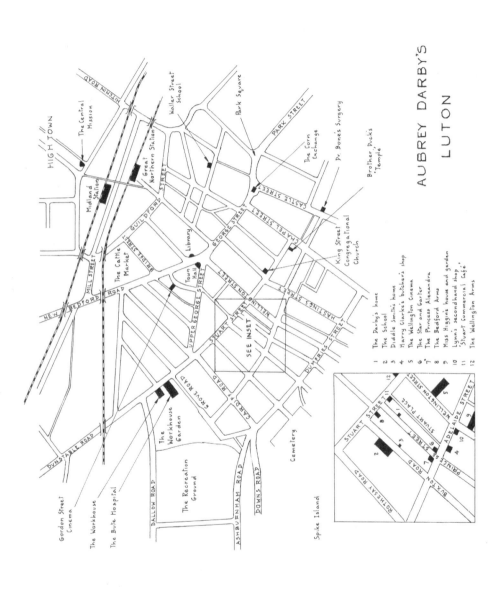

AUBREY DARBY'S
LUTON

HIGH TOWN

HITCHIN ROAD

The Central Mission

Midland Station

Great Northern Station

Waller Street School

Park Square

GUILDFORD STREET

STREET

Library

GEORGE STREET

PARK STREET

The Corn Exchange

CASTLE STREET

CHAPEL STREET

Dr. Bone's Surgery

Brother Ducks 'Temple'

King Street Congregational Church

The Cattle Market

BRISTOL STREET

Town Hall

UPPER GEORGE STREET

WELLINGTON STREET

STUART STREET

HASTINGS STREET

DUNSTABLE ROAD

MILL STREET

BEDFORD ROAD

NEW

The Workhouse Garden

GROVE ROAD

CARDIFF ROAD

DYERLS STREET

SEE INSET

Gordon Street Cinema

The Workhouse

The Bute Hospital

DALLOW ROAD

ASHBURNHAM ROAD

The Recreation Ground

DOWNS ROAD

Cemetery

Spike Island

1   The Darby's home
2   The School
3   Diddle Smith's home
4   Harry Clarke's butcher's shop
5   The Wellington Cinema
6   The Star and Garter
7   The Princess Alexandra
8   The Bedford Arms
9   Miss Higgins' house and garden
10 Lynn's secondhand shop
11 'Stuart Commercial Café'
12 The Wellington Arms

STUART STREET

BUXTON ROAD

ROTHESAY ROAD

PRINCE STREET

ADELAIDE STREET

STUART PLACE

WELLINGTON STREET

Children of Mary Ann Woodward (DARBY)

Herbert Goddard m. Mary Ann Woodward m. Walter Darby

Herbert Goddard
b. 1865
m. 1882 in Luton
d. 1895 in Luton

Mary Ann Woodward
b. 2 November 1862 in Flamstead, Hertfordshire
d. 1950 in Luton

Walter Darby
b. 1869 in Dunstable
m. 1895 in Luton
d. 1948 in Nottingham

Ernest Goddard	Emily Goddard	Gertrude Goddard	Gladys Goddard	Walter Darby	Frederick George Darby	Hettie Constance Darby	AUBREY SYDNEY DARBY
b. 1887	b. 1890	b. 1890	b. 1892	b. 1895	b. 1899	b. 1903	b. 1905
d. 1961	d. 1918	d. 1970	d. 1914	d. 1967	d. 1916	d. 1965	d. 1972

Walter, 46, and Mary Ann, 52, taken in 1914

I

My Life Begins

No star pinpointed the location of my birth, yet my father, who was drunk at the time, said it was a 'bloody miracle'. The old midwife, without conceding an immaculate conception, warned I would either be an imbecile or commit murder. Mother, aged forty-nine when I was born, and never guilty of looking a gift horse in the mouth, moved from the district, and knocked ten years off her age.

I never got to know Pa, he hopped it before I was old enough to recognise him; couldn't bear the sight of me, I suppose. Ma did say he was in politics, a friend of Joey Chamberlain, and almost a gentleman. I found out he had also been a soldier, through playing with his Boer War decorations, but they soon disappeared, flogged to make ends meet. An endowment left by my straying sire also ran out, compelling Ma to seek work. My age handicapped her, not yet old enough for school. Eventually she found a job in the hat trade, with me sitting beside her not daring to move, for fear the boss took umbrage and booted us out. Nine hours was a long time to sit inactive, and I looked forward to school. It could be no worse than this.

Edward was king, but it was still fashionable to wear black for Victoria. The globe was splashed with red, a gory reminder of our wealth and possessions, yet all our contemporaries were poverty stricken. The begetting of large families was the poor man's bromide, the pawnshop his bank, the pubs, allied to the pawnshops, dispensed strong ale, pepping up sires for the customary weekend bedding, an abundance of manure from horsedrawn traffic making this a time of great fertility.

Most working men voted Tory and considered organised labour unpatriotic. Wages of ten shillings for a sixty hour week were not uncommon, workers being summoned to work with the raucous blast of hooters and sirens. A dozen hooters blowing at 6:30 a.m. were enough to wake the dead. 'Hart's Whistle' with its high pitched tone silenced the morning songbirds.

Beer at a penny a pint called 'Porter' and bacca twopence a half-ounce were cheap, so was food, boiled bread pudding,

Dunstable Road looking from junction with Ivy Road 1907

suet pudding and treacle, sheep's-head stew, and meat clangers, filling the bellies of the poorest families.

Nothing seemed to change. All had a Sunday suit, worn only on that day and for funerals. Carefully preserved, it was also a source of income, pawned on Monday, redeemed on Saturday. We were all in the same boat: to have a job meant contentment, but apart from religious sects who called upon us to repent, my first impressions were of a wonderful world in which I would live forever.

The day I crossed the portals of the school destined to be my

63 Ivy Road - now modernised. Aubrey Darby spent the first six years of his life here - 1905-1911

only seat of learning, the rain poured down in sympathy with my depression. The academy blended with the squalid habitations surrounding it, and the bell perched on top like a carrion crow, tolled for us, and we learned to hate it.

Inside, two hundred and fifty boys squatted on backless forms, in uniforms of corduroys, tattered jerseys and handed down clobber; the few well-dressed boys, social outcasts, such was class distinction. We warmed to the sunlight, slanting down from narrow windows set high in the walls, highlighting the dust, and over all the assembly, a musty odour, peculiar to the environment.

The cane was a great persuader in hammering home how we were part of 'The Empire on which the sun never sets', kinsmen of the men who charged with the Light Brigade, and sons of the heroes who routed the Zulus. Progress was fairly rapid, only an imbecile could have failed to cope with a curriculum so sparse and insipid. The landed gentry always maintained that education made the peasants dissatisfied – our curriculum endorsed this philosophy.

In the wake of poverty charities inevitably trailed. The main source of income came ironically from the poor. The school 'Pound Day' was so named because we were expected to donate one pound in weight of any useful commodity, such as butter, bacon, tea etc. to the local hospital. Our lot contributed 200 lbs. of soda – soda was halfpenny per pound.

Food for the brain, we were getting that, but to fill the stomach Mother must work. In order not to interrupt her toil I was farmed out to 'Muff' Smith's family for meals. Muffy earned a living walking in front of the Council steam roller holding a red flag. The law decreed that a man should walk twelve paces ahead of the roller, holding the said banner. Mr. Smith's military bearing was very impressive, but the rear view was distorted by a large carbuncle protruding from the back of his neck like a tomato. Muffy was well in the public eye, but behind the scenes concocted herbal remedies guaranteed to cure everything from rheumatics to rickets. Scars on my right leg bear testimony to his cures when a six inch spike penetrated the shin bone. I would be ungrateful to suggest that I was dead lucky.

At this time the urge to make money dominated my life, so I found a job flogging newspapers. This was a lucrative business – on a good night I could make 4d. My education now broadened, pitting my wits against other boys bent on earning the magic lucre, and running like hell when caught on the bigger boys' territory. The word got round of the pickings to be had, and paper boys sprouted in the streets like candles on a conker tree. The market became saturated and I was out of work. It would take a long war to restore the profession to its former affluence.

Everyone pawned in the locality, but most had dignity and preferred to use pawnshop porters as go-betweens. This was a chance for me to get into business again. The duties of the porter were in the main collecting the old man's Sunday suit, blankets for sheets, and presenting them to the pawnbroker as security for hard cash, a kind of overdraft with security. Often the draught was felt in bed through the absence of bed clothes. The fee for porterage was 3d – my charge 2d – but this cut price was exorbitant when compared with the few coppers advanced by Uncle. There was no sentiment, this was business. The poor fed off the poor, the rich built walls to keep the cannibals out.

Business prospered, and I bought a pram to cart the growing bundles. Queen of the porters was an old crone known as Gran, who began to take a sinister interest in my progress. I underestimated her ability, and learned a lesson never to do that with anyone. She whispered a crafty word in the ear of my mother, and I was on the breadline again. Hot doughnuts and monkey nuts were out of reach. I saw nothing degrading in what I was doing. My own mother pawned, I reasoned, but she did not employ pawnshop labourers to do her dirty work. Mother's word was law and I argued no more.

Old Gran cornered the market in other professions out of my sphere. She was a free-lance midwife who advertised the fact by wearing a clean apron for the advent, an expert in birth control, crude but effective, and she prepared the departed for the ritual of lying-in-state. The best room, called the front room, was reserved for the corpse. In the centre of the room stood the open coffin on trestles, the lid leaning against the wall. Friends and neighbours filed in to take a last gawp at the deceased, complimenting the bereaved on how beautiful the body looked. Gran, as master of ceremonies, added to her patter by describing most reverently the place which the pitiable hulk was to inherit. Some of the more gullible were impatient to join the lucky one in Paradise.

2

My First Job

Unemployment and poverty were accepted as part of life, and at a time when a man could earn 12s 6d for a sixty hour week, employers found it more economical to employ two boys part-time at an individual wage of 2s 6d a week. The law, in its humanity, laid down that juveniles must be ten years old before qualifying for part-time work. This seemed stupid to me. I was now eight years old, and tried in some way to get round the law. From our front window I could read 'Dairy fed pork – Families catered for'. It was the local butcher's shop. I hung around the shop thinking of some excuse to speak to the butcher, and then, eureka! He asked me to fetch him a pennyworth of snuff, and I was in.

He refused my overtures at first, telling me I was too small, and not old enough in any case. For the reason of size I suggested standing on a box, finally clinching the job by offering my services not for a regular wage, but a tip now and then. Hours of work were 7:30 am to 8:30 am, mid-day when required, and in the evenings, 5:00 pm to 7:00 pm. Saturdays 7:30 am to 9.00 pm, and the final advice to remind him on Saturday night if he hadn't given me anything.

The butcher, like all the middle class, was religious, and one of my first errands was to cart a huge pumpkin he had grown to the Harvest Festival. I became acquainted with new smells as butcher boy, but from the beginning, the sickly sweet scent of snuff he pushed up his nostrils nauseated me.

All butchers owned their own slaughter houses, cattle on the hoof were inspected at the market, but 'midnight' butchering never was. Often animals died on a farm, through calving or from colic. The butcher was quickly on the scene, and late at night the animal, now gutted and de-blooded, was finally dressed in the slaughter house. Only the expert could know that the beast had died an unnatural death. Bladders of water, adhering to the inside of the rib cage, were a sign of tuberculosis. A sponge down removed the evidence, and no one was the wiser. Cancerous growths and tumours on pigs were cut away, and the butcher eased his conscience by selling the meat a copper or two cheaper. Saturday night auction of left-over meat was a popular feature of the trade, meat cunningly displayed to hide unsavoury fat and gristle, was handled incessantly by the choosy housewife. Constant mauling of the meat had one great advantage: it disturbed the blow flies bent on using the joints as a nursery for future offspring.

My first Christmas in the trade was a nightmare. All poultry was bought live, and the week before the festive day we worked from dusk until midnight every night, plucking and gutting the birds. Candle-lit barns and the restless crowing and fighting of the caged poultry, feathers flying all about were macabre enough, but we were tormented with the fleas, extra vicious in being parted from the warmth of their feathered friends. After a time fingers became raw and cramped, but always we raced against time. Pheasant plucking was a foul operation, the birds were 'high', peppered with shot and putrid. We who tugged the feathers from the rotten carcasses thought them inedible, but the people who ate them were our social superiors. Who were we to offer an opinion?

By late Christmas Eve we were left only with the tidying up and de-lousing. In gratitude for our achievements the butcher regaled us with beer and sandwiches. After closing the shop he gave us our pay, and a little extra for Christmas. My extra was a brace of wood pigeons, good exercise for the jawbone but hardly digestible.

Logically, a man who is kind to animals is a good man. The love my boss showered upon his horse put him in the category of a saint. This over-fed, underworked, vicious brute often took a nip at my backside when I was curry-combing him. One day the beast took a piece out of the slaughter-man's posterior. He, whose job it was to destroy animals, promptly kicked the horse in the ribs. Unfortunately for him, the boss saw him do it, and a few days later a new slaughterer appeared. Prince, the regal name by which the horse was known, enjoyed six weeks holiday every summer, turned out to grass on a farm. While he was away we humped the meat around on 'Shanks' Pony'. When the horse returned we still walked, leading him by the bridle, otherwise the beast would have taken us back to his green pastures.

3

The Butcher Boys

Tempus fugit. Now I was ten years-old, legally on the pay roll at a salary of 3s 6d a week, and accepted by the brotherhood of butcher boys in the town. The master butchers encouraged the boys to help each other out with such chores as lard boiling and sausage making. We relieved the boredom of sausage filling with pelting each other with the sausage meat. None was wasted: the mess adhering to the walls was cleared off and returned to the filling machine.

Residue from lard boiling was a crisp mess of skin and gristle called 'crinklings'. These were our perks to be given away or sold. When possible we charged a penny for a basinful. One mean old dear by-passed us and got the boss to give us orders to deliver a load to her residence buckshee every week. We countered this by urinating in her basinful. The plan misfired: she told the butcher that last week's crinklings were more tasty than ever.

Wednesday was half-day closing and on Sunday, after feeding the horse, I was free until bedding him down. Leisure time in the week was spent at the pictures, one of the two palaces named after the great soldiers Wellington and Gordon. If the picture palaces were any criterion, these two must have been a crumby pair. We paid 2d to sit on hard forms, with bare boards underfoot, our necks craned at an acute angle looking upwards at a flickering, not too silvery screen.

Some of the cheap-seat patrons must have been loose watered, judging by the wetness soaking through our thin boots. The pianist, Blue Nose, had a restricted repertoire of two melodies *The Rustle of Spring* and *Teddy Bear's Picnic*. During the performance he frequently visited The Bladder of Lard opposite the cinema to wet his whistle. Around 10 pm when the villain was about to strangle the heroine it was not unusual for him to serenade the audience with the pastoral *Rustle of Spring* when he should have been thundering out *If you go down to the woods today*. The chucker out was 'Tin Ribs' who rigidly enforced the rules of no nut cracking and no fish and chips to be consumed on the premises. When we brought chips in, he would nose his way along the seats and smell out the culprit. We fooled him some of the time by indignantly protesting that we ate them before we came in.

Wednesday night was Mafeking Night for butcher boys, the one time in the week when we could really be free to enjoy life. Once we were cheated. The advertised film was *Custer's Last Stand* and, our appetite whetted by the posters, we turned out in force, paid our money and raced down the gangway in order to get the best seats. The dimly lit palace darkened still more, and on the screen appeared Lilian Gish in a torrid love drama. There was no justice, they had cheated us, so we created pandemonium.

The lights went up, Lilian disappeared from the screen and down stalked Tin Ribs. 'Any more of this and out you go,' he shouted. This had no effect. He retired and appeared again with the manager, who usually occupied his time by managing the skirt in the box office. Very politely Casanova told how the advertised epic had been mislaid on the rail and with what great expense he had got a substitute film.

We quietened after his oration and once more Miss Gish started her necking lark. It was too much, we didn't appreciate the love game: blood and thunder was our cup of tea. We pelted the screen with everything we could find and it split under the bombardment. That was our exit, slung out and banned for ever; no return money either.

We transferred our patronage to the lesser fleapit, and for a time enjoyed a cut-price entertainment. One boy would pay to go in, and at a convenient moment slip the bar at the emergency exit. The rest of us crawled in on hands and knees for a free seat. We were never able to work this at Tin Rib's emporium because the emergency exit didn't function. The chucker out at our cut price cinema sported a club foot, but he moved very quickly on the night he tumbled to our dodge. Now we were really out, literally on the streets.

Monday was cattle market day when butchers and animal lovers assembled, either to buy cattle or take a morbid interest in the proceedings. Massive Herefords, dainty maiden heifers, sheep and pigs, were driven to the auction ring to be prodded and felt by the experts. The auctioneer, peering down from his rostrum like a brooding vulture, chanted away like a Tibetan priest, before banging his hammer down and squawking, 'Done.' Then the drover whacked the bewildered beast away from its tormentors. A condemned murderer was given a last meal, but these animals were not fed, empty stomachs made disembowelling easier. Were the gormandisers, who stuffed themselves on the flesh of these poor beasts, made to witness this revolting spectacle, more would become vegetarian.

The job of delivering the cattle on the hoof to the scattered slaughter houses rested with Bowler, the head drover. This loud mouthed character was as arrogant as a bullfighter, tattered smock and big stick substituting for cape and sword. The beef all sold, sixty head of cattle in one great steaming herd lurched out of the market into the streets, Bowler hollering instructions above the din. Women screamed and grown men flinched as the cavalcade thundered on, the bellowing was a descant to the drover's cry, the hoof beats like muted drums. Now the cry, 'Steadyem',

Gordon Street Cinema. The chucker out is to the rear on the right of the photograph. He was W.J. Edwards, later Mayor of Luton

as the cattle threaded through the horse-drawn traffic, and the curse of 'Bloody Bullocks' was in the air. Away from the hostile traffic, up the hill into the becalmed side street, the herd settled into a steady gait, and still - castrated steers mounted the backs of maiden heifers, as though all were not yet lost. Into the alleys where the slaughterhouses lurked, and the command, 'Get in front Boy, hold 'em.'

Now a sea of horns on the flood tide milled and circled before coming to rest, and the magic of Bowler manifested itself when he conjured one animal, the right one, from the mass, and coaxed it into the death chamber. The herd moved on, resting here and there until the last animal, frantically bawling for its departed kin, was finally disposed of. It was to be death in the afternoon but the matador had played his part.

Back tracking through the inevitable trail of dung, it was to be the turn of the sheep. Bowler's status did not allow for sheep droving, so the underlings took over with what pandemonium! Without the authority of Bowler we were all in charge, the sheep sensing this, scattered in all directions. Every opening and alleyway was invaded and all the time the bleating of the woollies drove us crackers. Unlike the noble beef, these animals were stupid, and we felt more stupid as we chased all over the shop after them. Any sympathy we may have had for their impending doom evaporated as the crowd of kids following us, delighting at our predicament, chased the sheep further afield. Nevertheless the impossible was achieved and the 'Baa Lambs' safely home.

Now for the pigs – and for this exacting task Bowler again became master of ceremonies. The pig drive was a delicate affair, for at the softest touch they squealed loud and long. Onlookers who saw in pork some affinity with themselves would soon take up the cudgel on their behalf had they thought we were ill-treating them. Were they to see the method of slaughter when the pig's throat was cut whilst fully conscious, then the animal get to its feet and walk around while the blood gushed, they could justifiably protest. As it was, the porkers en route to the slaughter house had to be treated gently because the slightest knock brought out severe bruising on the dressed carcass.

Tired out, and smelling to high heaven, Bowler dished out the coppers for services rendered, and we dispersed past the scurrying lamplighter, busy lighting up the darkening streets. Today we were too weary to shin up lamp-posts and turn out the lights; this day the lamplighter laboured not in vain.

Rain would cleanse the polluted streets. Till then feet would carry the odour into the inner recesses of homes en route of the departed herds.

4

The Life Around Me

Whilst flogging newsprint I only had the eyes for customers, now, as a freelance, most things animate and inanimate seemed worthy of attention. Consumptives, cripples, halfwits, drunks, and even pink-eyed albinos, of which there were four families in Luton, graced the horse-dung littered streets. Flies abounded and fly-papers stuck-to with their protesting victims, added a kind of music in the shops of the hygienic minded vendors of foodstuffs. Beggars requested a copper for a bite to eat, and religious cranks foretold the coming of the Lord. After viewing this lot, no doubt He would then return from whence He came.

Odd characters gave colour to the grey vista, and one such, being 'Liquor Sharpe', performed regularly for our edification. When sober he sold soiled headgear, delving down into a sack before bringing forth various hats to tickle the fancy of my ladies. The titfers were remarkably cheap. When drunk, Liquor waged a vendetta with a local baker. Then it was he put on his regalia: adorning his chest was a life-sized portrait of his mother, at the rear a portrait of his father, a kind of sandwich board effect. Parading the streets, like a Pied Piper without music, he gathered in his wake a multitude of kids who knew the drill.

Finally, he stood outside the baker's shop and prayed for silence. 'Old So and So, Seducer of Women – one old whore in

High Town, one old whore in Park Street – dirty old sod!' Then we all cheered, and beseeched him to say it again. This went on and on until the Police carted Liquor, portraits and hats, into the lock-up. Usually he got away with seven days.

Sunday was strictly observed as the Sabbath, the only activity coming from Pub and Pulpit. For our Sunday amusement we relied on the Salvation Army, which, when the weather was kind, held mass open-air meetings in the town centre. Crowds flocked to listen to the band; the evangelists were tolerated as an overture.

After the service came the scrounging, when the audience were cajoled into tossing money on to the big drums, craftily placed in the centre of the arena. This was where we came in, pelting the taut skin with every conceivable bit of rubbish we could lay our hands on. If the crowd turned on us, then the seeker after souls knew he had been successful in his efforts. However, we had that one essential asset of the urchin, fleetness, so we came to no harm.

One Sunday, a new Messiah appeared in the streets, none other than Mr. Duck, the erstwhile pawnshop clerk. Whilst on holiday he had seen the light, and now, garbed in flowing gown and shaggy beard, he had gathered round himself twelve disciples, housing them in an old paint shop he had rented in a back street. A number of his disciples were known to us – 'Polly Lookup', who because of a neck stricture was for ever condemned to look heavenwards, Bert of the club foot and withered hand, Alfie, who exposed his penis and sang 'Gentle Jesus, Meek and Mild' on request, and Billy Bottoms, a simpleton, whose only vice was to take buckets of water and a scrubbing brush to any empty premises he saw, and clean them from attic to cellar. For these foul deeds Billy was put into an asylum.

Mr. Duck, now calling himself 'Mr. Duck the Chosen', extracted sufficient money from these pitiful souls to keep him without working. The sight of this motley crew, shuffling along the streets prior to the meeting, was sufficient to send us into fits of hysterical mirth. When at last they entered the Temple we waited until they were on their knees, before creeping in and bellowing, 'Brother Duck, Quack, Quack, Quack!' We had no respect for the new Messiah but in our peculiar manner, thought we were assisting his disciples.

Charlie Irons, the Town Crier, was a joy to behold. Over six feet tall, a green top hat accentuated his height, with waxed moustaches, far reaching. The majesty of this Herculean figure was awe inspiring to the uninitiated, but we knew him for what he was, a crafty old hypocrite, who commanded small boys to carry his heavy bell, too idle himself to hump his symbol

of office. Charlie, like all the upper class, was religious, a Salvationist in fact, who delighted in wrecking other denominational services by proclaiming 'Hallelujah' and 'God be Praised,' just when the preacher was expounding profound utterances. The foghorn of a voice inevitably stopped the preacher in his tracks, when Charlie would commence to preach his idea of religion.

'Keeper of the Pound' was one of the Town Crier's titles, whereby all stray animals were kept for a period in the pound, a large shed kept for the purpose. Charlie kept the key, fed the strays and levied heavy charges on those who claimed their animals. We came up with an idea for making capital gain, by 'finding' nine sheep before they were lost, simply by opening a gate where they were grazing, and shooing them into the road.

Charles Irons
Town Crier and
Keeper of the Pound

Inevitably it was Sunday, fine and warm, and more than the usual number of worshippers were on the way to church, when four scruffy urchins drove nine potential rewards through the main street and up the hill to the residence of Charlie Irons Esquire, Town Crier, Keeper of the Pound.   If that was not enough, 'Mount Tabor' also described the abode. We knocked on the door, and were told to wait until Mr. Irons came home from the service. Wait we did, for two hours, and all this time the patient flock were fouling the pavement and treading the muck into a thick, dark brown carpet.

Then Charlie appeared in the distance. We knew him from a mile away, and we rehearsed the story again. He of the Hallelujah chorus for once was speechless, but, finally digesting what we were saying, he exploded with abuse, even calling the sheep droppings by a rude name. Sunday or not, he had to do his duty, so four boys and nine sheep followed the Keeper of the Pound to the place where the animals would be housed and fed, pending claimant. He wrote down our addresses, and we departed in high spirits. We had been assured that we would be rewarded.

Three months later, and after repeated pestering of Charlie Irons for our reward, my mother answered a knock on the door, and in strode the gentleman who was to make us rich. 'Sign here, Madam,' commanded Charlie, extracting sixpence from a jug purse. All along my mother had been sceptical of the amount of reward forthcoming, but even she was stunned by the paltry sixpence, and told Mr. Irons in no small manner what a damned old rogue he was. The tirade left Moneybags unmoved, and he left our midst with a courteous, 'Good – day, Madam.'

Nearing Yuletide our thoughts turned to carols, for there was cash in this lark. One mouth organ, a carriage lamp we 'found', a candle bought, and we were equipped. We sang 'Good King Wenceslas' at every house; it was easy to sing and we knew all the words. Our clients were the elite, there was no future in the common herd. By some instinct or intuition we always avoided the large residence of Mr. Bird, a big business man who subscribed lavishly to most charities. This year we decided to try him out, and appeared on his porch. Throats cleared, we sang in dulcet tones, no mucking about, but serious. We came to 'Ye who now do bless the poor shall yourselves find blessing' – and then bashed on his ornate knocker. The great man himself opened the door and gazed benevolently upon us. 'Very nicely sung, boys, excellent, and for what charity do you wish me to make a cheque?'

Alas, for once we were not quick witted enough, and the mouth organist answered, 'We're singing for ourselves, Sir.' Now the smile went from the face of the great benefactor.

Major Payne

'I only give to the recognised charities.'

'But we are the poor in need of charity.'

'Be off before I phone the police,' was all we got out of him. Our intuition was not to be ignored in the future.

Easter to us meant hot cross buns. A month prior to Good Friday we touted for orders. 'Buns, hot smoking hot, delivered in time for breakfast!' We got two quids worth of orders, not bad when considering buns were ten for threepence. Next we persuaded the baker to let us have the buns on 'tick' at five shillings in the pound discount.

Six thirty a.m. Good Friday, buns pressed flat in bath tubs and clothes baskets, were loaded on to the hat barrow designed for carrying hat boxes, but liable to tip up if the load was not evenly distributed. We set off with our street cry – 'all hot, smoking hot!' – waking the slumbering clients. Banging on the door knockers with soggy lumps of dough we waited for the expected criticism because the buns were stone cold and the crosses obliterated. However, they sold, if not like hot cakes, until catastrophe: half the load was despatched, and the barrow handles had to be sat on. We overlooked this, with the result that the load tipped up and buns cascaded into the wet road. We salvaged most, by wiping them on our jackets and trousers, but sold no more in that locality – we knew that they were a fussy lot anyway.

5

The Free Breakfast

On Good Friday invitations went out to attend the free breakfast. To qualify for the meal one must be the offspring of poor parents. So a multitude of children gathered outside the Congregational Church. Inside, the elders prepared the feast. The Church, a massive structure of grey stone, was noted for its high steeple, and gazing aloft we imagined the spire would fall down upon us before we could crowd into the depths of the crypt.

Breakfast was a bowl of porridge, an orange, a bun and much salt to flavour the 'skilly', the providers believing this repast would sustain us on the road to salvation. We showed our appreciation by flicking the manna in all directions, like the pauper's lament over his Christmas pudding. If we were to accept charity, something more substantial than a bellyful of porridge would have to be forthcoming. Before the feast we chanted, 'May the Lord make us truly thankful,' most evident after the telling of the Crucifixion, when we stormed up the stone stairs into the warmth of a cold Good Friday morning.

The mournful day was paradise to the believers: two Sundays in one week; purgatory for the rest who risked damnation in an effort to seek happiness on the extra day free from toil. A day of penance when all ate fish according to his means. Cod's head or Scotch salmon, protocol must be observed. If poverty be a passport to heaven, then he who fasted on broken bloaters merited more favour in the eyes of the all-seeing. Poor consolation to the alley cat foraging in the dustbin; fish offal merited no place in the hereafter for him.

The day lingered on, the echo of that death in the dim past encompassing small boys in moments of gloom. So much so, that householders were spared the torments of 'Knock up Ginger', standby for bored urchins. We waited for the evening and the Magic Lantern when the Methodists would describe by word and picture the evils of strong drink. Hot cross buns would be distributed as another inducement, further constipating our dough-filled stomachs.

The Methodist Church, on top of the hill overlooking the railway sidings, stood four square, no spike, no ornamental masonry, symbolising a narrowness personified from within that only the poor needed saving, the rich being blessed by the Lord. Inside the hall, gaslit and shabby, sat rows of children gazing at a white screen, from which light and colour would soon emerge. As the minutes ticked by from a large clock on the wall, a restlessness became apparent, breaking out into loud cheers with the appearance of the Pastor on the platform. Did he know our cheers were for the imminent showing of the pictures heralded by his entry? If not, we left him in no doubt, when halfway through his address, the cry, 'Show the pictures,' led to the exit of a chastened cleric.

The hall darkened and the first slide appeared upside down, accompanied by screams of laughter and catcalls. There was Mafeking everywhere. Right way up, the picture, in magnificent colour, depicted a filthy attic. The occupants were a repulsive woman in rags and two scarecrows, barefoot, presumably her children, peering at a crust of bread reposing on the rickety table, the scene highlighted by a candle stuck in a beer bottle, seemed to us who had experience of this kind of illumination remarkably bright, for every detail of the sordid room stood out clearly.

The storyteller interpreting the scene told us the family were waiting for the father to come home with his pay, but the demon strong drink had waylaid him. The slide changed, showing the drunken father, red choker round his neck, in the act of bashing the wife, whilst the kids cowered in a corner. The compere, warming up to his job, carried the cackle a bit too far, so we shouted for the next picture. The excitement of the imminent bashing fired our imagination, the plight of the victims worried us not. So the story unfolded, the droning voice of the story teller lulling many of us to sleep. Some even lost interest in something all so true to life in this age of pub and pulpit. Those who watched to the bitter end saw the drunken swine repent, but only after his only son had been knocked over by a runaway horse and cart. The final scene, a beautiful room, the son between snow-white sheets, well-dressed father, wife and daughter smiling down upon the happy boy, and in the background the pastor kneeling in act of prayer. In some strange way we wondered why the runaway horse received no credit for the happy ending.

In our world of reality, neither the magic lantern nor the religious man convinced us that strong drink or total abstinence would change our existence. Religion was alien to our environment, for what purpose we lived no one cared. Living was enough, mysticism had no abode in our attics. We had no education and believed those who craved after it were cranks. Nevertheless, after the Lantern Show we were content, the herd instinct of being together, a free bun, a warm hall, and the joy of the upside down picture had satisfied our expectations. Our fathers would still visit the pubs and for this fact we said, 'Amen.'

Homeward bound, more subdued with the cold night than the Magic Lantern, we passed some of the ninety pubs in town. Tonight, the soft murmur of voices denoted peace in the pubs. There were no raucous brawls, and we wondered who could have done this thing. We looked into the starlit sky, shivered, and scampered home.

6

The Stattie

Come Easter Monday, with great expectations, this was Stattie day, a new heaven, for the fish day had passed away. Ancient byelaws decreed that showmen, quack doctors, gypsies and diverse twilight characters could erect their paraphernalia in the main streets. The Statute Fair, the official title, further befouled the highways, much to the annoyance of the opposition, but we were in power on this day so the soul seekers stayed away.

Outside the Corn Exchange, men joyfully hurled wooden balls at coconuts artfully wedged into cup-shaped receptacles perched on sticks, very similar to the peg legs of Boer War veterans. The roundabouts, showpiece of the fair, held pride of place near the 'Pepper Box', a nickname for the memorial to an alleged town benefactor.

It was possible to free-ride the mechanical monster by nipping on to the revolving platform after the fare collector had passed. If caught we received a bashing, poor reward for risking our limbs on up and down painted horses, travelling round in circles. The swinging boats were a swindle, we never free-rode them, were never able to pull high enough on the red woolly ropes. Men preferred to take girls for a go and it was very difficult for the females to control billowing skirts, whilst clinging to the ropes of the high riding boats.

GEORGE STREET. LUTON.

George Street with The Corn Exchange in the background

The rockmaker, conjurer of 'spit rock', held court at the entrance to the public lavatory, production of the rock being a long, drawn-out work of art. First, a dark brown lump, dough-like in texture, was thumped and kneaded. Then, from bottles of varying colours, liquid was poured slowly on to the mass. Holding each bottle in turn up to the view of the crowd, he would single out one of them: 'You, Madam – this is the nectar of the gods – for you a taste of paradise.' Then selecting another bottle – 'You, Madam – this potion will bless you with many children,' a remark causing much belly laughter. Obviously he had picked out a woman, the victim of over production!

Came the miracle: tossing the lump of soft rock over a large hook, the Rockman spat on his hands and pulled the rock into skeins. Over and over the hook looped the rock, until, before our eyes the hardening rock turned from brown to creamy white. As the magician chopped the rock into penny lumps trade was brisk, and small boys in the forefront grabbed the splinters of rock left on the slab, warily watching the descending chopper in the process.

No pickings were possible at the sausage and bread stall, but the warmth of the coke brazier, over which the sausages sizzled in a large pan, was good reason for lingering round the stall. When trade was good, the sausages were served up half cooked; when trade was bad, the 'jerks' were done to death.

The 'Painless Dentist' attracted a large audience, morbid and sadistic in the tradition of a public execution. Stooges were bribed to walk about the crowd, testifying to the dentist's skill. Then the great man made his appearance in top hat and cutaway frockcoat, claiming to be a noted surgeon, who, from the kindness of his heart, descended into the market place to cure the poor of their bad teeth. Soon the first patient appeared on the platform and was asked to point out, with his finger, the offending molar. The stooges surrounded the patient, and the dentist, grasping what looked like pliers in his ham-like fist, dived into the gaping mouth, and with lightning speed and brute force tore the tooth out before the shock had registered on the brain of the victim. Holding the molar aloft, he focused all attention upon himself whilst the cronies extracted a shilling from the patient, assuring him or her that the tooth would ache no more.

We gazed in awe at the quack doctors dispensing potions guaranteed to cure every ailment, and desperately ill people paying out money for coloured liquids with a blind faith bordering on imbecility. In those days iodine was the main germicide and 'blue stone', a kind of caustic stick, was used to burn away dead tissue: a vicious circle with iodine destroying flesh and 'blue stone' burning it away. Appendicitis was called inflammation of the bowels, often developing into peritonitis. King Edward V11 had been stricken with the ailment, when necessity to save the monarch made the medical profession find a cure through surgery.

In daylight the Stattie was obscene, with nightfall it seemed like Dante's Inferno. Flickering lights from kerosene flares haloed in smoke made an unearthly glow, inanimate objects came to life, and the faces of the revellers appeared like the gargoyles of Notre Dame. In this setting the appearance of Quasimodo would have evoked no surprise. Away from the glare, whores entertained any male with fourpence to spare, plagued at times by peeping toms seeking a cheap thrill. Syphilis was common but none cared on Stattie night. The raucous din of machine-made music muffled the whimperings of tiny tots being dragged around by wretched mothers bent on escaping from reality. Tomorrow they would account for the squandering of precious wealth on sideshows, tonight they laughed and squealed with ecstasy, whilst grown men emptied water squirts down their breasts. All inhibitions were gone, young virgins satisfied their curiosity, and 'Knees up old Ma Brown' was an excuse for matrons to expose a gartered thigh.

Toward the last hour drunks spewed from the pubs, finale to

the hectic day, and like the titbit left on the plate until last, how we savoured this morsel. Fights broke out everywhere, and we scurried here and there, alert for overturned stalls. Diving into the wreckage we grabbed all we could lay our hands on, before departing into the shadows with our loot. The appearance of the bobbies, the frogmarch of the drunks to the lockup, was of little interest to us. We could see all this on any Saturday night.

7

Men About Town

On the morning following the Stattie, Albert strolled through the town, attired in frocktail coat, green with envy, tatty plus-fours, and ammunition boots shining with Reckitt's grate polish. His headgear of bowler hat somewhat spoilt the ensemble, but Mad Albert, giving him his full title, paraded with the confidence of one who was noticed. He was a much-travelled man, having done service for many years with the army in India, life under the Indian sun leaving him the double legacies of ague and 'dullali'. The bouts of shivering played havoc with Albert's lean frame, the spells of madness coinciding with the moon's changes. Self-styled champion of the oppressed and philosopher, Albert believed that beggars could be choosers, silencing his critics with acid wit and biting tongue.

Today he noted the yard-wide bass brooms, iron barrows, the casual labourers and the mountain of litter left over from the fair. He noted with jaundiced eye the regular scavengers bullying the casuals into working harder than they could ever match themselves, and cried out against little men in brief authority. 'Rise up you scum and destroy your taskmasters,' raved Albert, but the slaves jeered Albert more than the oppressors. Albert, who was mad, went on his way, pondering and brushing that which was unclean from his person, met Rosie and rejoiced.

Rosie, called Tuppenny Tube, was a prostitute, and Albert, in his role of protector, shielded the whore from the riff-raff who condemned her. He revered Rosie with a devotion far removed from intercourse. She, in return, offering Woodbines, readily accepted by Albert without thought of how they were obtained. It mattered not that this affinity could be likened to drunkenness and poverty, Albert crying out loud against religious bodies who pestered the authorities to rid the streets of his beloved Rosie. Indeed Albert was in jeopardy of being put away, save only that no relatives came forward to sign the papers.

So Albert continued his walk, pausing now to admire the railway dray- horses, noble beasts, well fed, well groomed and adorned with shining brasses, exciting the envy of lesser mortals who would change places with such harnessed elegance. On to the railway station, and here Albert ceremoniously buckled to his arm the proud insignia 'Midland Railway' in red letters on a black background, signifying to the world at large that he, Mad Albert, had permission to solicit bona fide travellers having luggage, after leaving the station.

Free-lance porter Albert contracted to carry the luggage to any destination, be it the waiting hansom cab or to the abode of the traveller. The tip, twopence or two shillings, was graciously accepted, for Albert always maintained he was of independent means. During the hot summers of school holidays, we talked to Albert of many things, and listened with rapt attention to his tales of India. The story of the tired Punka Wallah was like something from the Decameron Nights. On rare occasions we were privileged to help carry baggage, walking at a respectful distance behind his fare. Tactfully, Albert explained that scruffy urchins like us would embarrass his clients. Philosopher, Wit, Protector of the Poor, Albert succumbed to the fashionable disease of the time, consumption, and was buried in the paupers' cemetery – plain deal coffin and unconsecrated ground – signifying to the public that the parish had interred him.

'Who ate the dog's dinner?' - 'Scallions!' with question and answer to our greeting for the repulsive figure of the rascally ragbone man. His street cry of 'Bone, Bone,' monotonously intoned in a squeaking voice, causing us to drop what mischief we were about in an endeavour to get him to chase us. Despite never being successful he always obliged, and we gloried in the chase. Round the block, always a few yards behind us, Scallions and a horde of boys scooted, and as he fell further behind we had time to tip his junk barrow on end. Pausing to right his barrow he hurled foul language at us. Protesting women, forgetting they often used the same language when abusing us, upbraided him for his filthy tongue, and Scallions, like a stag at bay, roared with anguish.

None knew Scallions' real name, no one claimed relationship; his address 'No Fixed Abode', and he dossed at the fourpenny doss house, known as 'The Welcome Stranger'. He seemed to make a good living from ragboning, mainly through intimidation, scared housewives parting with rags to be rid of him. Many tales were told about him, the most persistent of his requesting to use the toilet of a local barber. Asked by the barber who shaved him, Scallions replied, 'I shave myself.' The punch line, 'You can go and --- yourself!' resulted in much mirth.

Often he would be carrying puppy dogs and kittens on his barrow, and my one transaction in buying a pup off him led to a companionship with an animal I dearly loved. It could be that this man, the butt of small boys, liked animals, and offered shelter to the unwanted ones. If so, our baiting of him was unworthy.

Small boys can be cruel, unwittingly, and in later years the baiting of Scallions has given me some uneasiness. Here was a man, repulsive – yes, unwashed, unshaven, yet he made a living, undaunted by boys who must have driven him to desperation with their pranks. I would like to think that Scallions, being a man alone, played up to us, and entered into the spirit of our game, not wanting to be a spoilsport. Be it so, I shall never know.

Of all the characters in the town, Bang-Bang gave us least excitement. Summer and winter, no matter what the weather, he took up position from daybreak until dusk, outside The Bedford Arms, wearing at least three overcoats. A greying beard haloed his face, matted and spread as if he had stuck his head through a crow's nest. Two beady eyes searched the horizon, and his nose, like an unbaked cottage loaf, was for ever dew- dropped. His feet, bound up in rags, were encased in boots more holey than righteous, and the protruding rags suggested the winged feet of a mythical Greek god. One foot pressed back on to the pub wall, suggested the trademark of a Soho whore.

How Bang-Bang survived was a mystery, never seen to work, he always fed well, delving into his many pockets at noon to bring forth huge lumps of bread and fat belly pork. So regular was his midday feast that people remarked, 'It must be gone twelve, Bang-Bang's grubbing.' Molest him? We did, mainly in winter with snow about, but even spot target snowballs failed to rouse him. Unlike the sporting Scallions, he was never one for the chase. We were never able to move him, dumb insolence making a mockery of all our unworthy efforts. At dusk he shuffled off with a limping gait. We followed him once, right to the outskirts of the town, but with the darkening sky, gave up and left the night to Bang-Bang.

One day Bang-Bang was missing from his accustomed pitch, and some concern was felt. It was unfair, he was part of our life, like school and hot cross buns. Questions were asked; we even asked a bobby if he had seen him and got more than a negative reply. So the weeks slipped by, and the picture of Bang-Bang became a little faded, when a cry, 'They have found him!' echoed round the playground. True, they had found him – dead, with his face half eaten away by rats. His last resting place an old barn, unmourned except by us, his tormentors. We would sorrow for him in our fashion, and have nightmares after discussing his awful death.

8

The Italians

The Italian community were self supporting, versatile and hard-working, becoming organ grinders, ice-cream vendors, hot-pea merchants and roast chestnut purveyors, according to season. An elite few were fine craftsmen, specialising in mosaics and the shaping of composition hat blocks. They were a volatile people, excitable and gay, lending a deal of colour to the town. The older generation never really mastered the English language, and when 'Wet weather' called us 'bloody fukky monkeys,' she was unaware of any obscenity.

Wetweather was an old Italian woman who stumped the streets with a barrel organ, never forsaking her Italian dress. She had jet-black hair, enhanced by gold earrings, and wore the traditional fringed head-shawl patterned in chocolate and green. A wide belt round her middle held in place skirt and underskirts of various shades, so back or front she always looked pregnant. The long skirt almost hid buttoned boots of shiny black leather, but when she rested her foot on the wheel of the barrel organ, the boots allowed just a peep at her red stockings. Eyes like liquorice peered from behind a hooked nose of great length, her wide mouth compensating for the affliction. Skin the colour of Christmas pudding completed the portrait, reconcilable with an aged Mona Lisa. We believed the legend that she made it rain, hence her name, Wetweather. We thought she was a witch and rarely pestered her. When we did, it was to chant from afar, 'Wetweather, Wetweather, go away, make it rain another day!'

The ice-cream man, with his gaily painted ice-cream barrow dispensed dollops of 'hokey' from metal tubs surrounded with ice, delving with a wooden spatula, emerging with the concoction and scraping it on a bone-hard cornet or wafer. The hokey was gritty with particles of ice added to give bulk, and the 'cream' could never have originated from a cow's udder. Nevertheless, we licked away at it. The portion was generous, it was cold and sweet, only knocked us back a ha'penny, so who cared.

The hurdy-gurdy man: most appreciated was he with the monkey. The little animal, decked out in velvet coat and tasselled cap, was wide eyed and sorrowful, tethered to a long chain. It was taught to go round with the hat. Armed with orange peel and apple cores, we quickly filled it, the monkey with squeaks of delight retreating to the end of the chain and wolfing down the freely given fruit. The organ man, gesticulating with rage all the time, tried to pinch the titbits off the animal, the monkey making loud ticking noises. With one hand apparently glued to the handles, the monkey man continued to grind out the classic, with the 'show must go on' complex, whilst we chuckled and jigged to the music. Finally he gave up, grabbed the monkey and shuffled away, lugging the cumbersome music maker after him.

The roast-chestnut man who took up his station in the alley at the rear of a pub was very popular, the proceeds of a returned empty bottle ensuring hours of warm glow, basking in the heat from his fire. Even when it rained we kept dry under the corrugated sheet, spread over the stall. We imagined ourselves out west, camping with a wagon train, an illusion not shared by the chestnut roaster, who forever yarned about his beloved Italy. He was a young man, born in England, first generation of Italian parents, who spoke little English and were ambitious to make lira, go home, and buy a vineyard. The chestnut man, a devout

Catholic, spoke of his parents with great respect, always referring to them as Mama and Papa, promising that one day he would take us home to meet them. We never expected that he would invite us, until one bitterly cold night, with a gale blowing, he packed up his stall earlier than usual. Ignoring our protests, he said, 'Go home, this weather is much too cold.' Then, scribbling his address on a piece of paper, he told us to visit him on the following Sunday afternoon. 'Perhaps Mama will give you tea, and Papa show you our factory,' he said, lugging the wind-swept fire and barrow out from the alley. We followed him for part of the way, and only gave up when he burst into Italian, leaving us in no doubt that chestnut flogging was finished for the night.

On the Sunday, four of us set off and kept faith with our Italian friend. The house, situated in the poorest district, was on a par with our own homes, but the welcome from Mama and Papa was all-embracing. Even Papa hugged us, our friend beaming at us, whilst a number of small children stood in respectful silence waiting to be introduced. The living room was crammed with religious pictures, statues and Victorian bric-a-brac, a huge fire in the grate making the room warm and colourful. Then Papa got a word in, and ushered us out the back door to inspect the factory.

The factory, a wooden shed with varied extensions, was entered from a door bearing the description, 'No admittance except on business', making us feel important as we strolled in. It was a dirt floor imprinted with the marks of a pony's hoofs, the pony standing in one corner munching hay. A barrel organ had pride of place, Papa proudly showing us the walnut veneer, attached shafts for pony hauling and the elegant harness. He assured us that many Sunday School outings and festivals far out of town were able to hear his music, because of his shafted organ and pony. The ice-cream factory was a let down, consisting of various bowls and pails. A large funnel, a sieve and a tub with propeller inside worked by a large handle.

'The ice-cream she is closed for the winter,' the old man explained, guiding us past the roast chestnut contraption already prepared for the morrow. Then he stopped at a screened off section and gabbled away in Italian to us that we were about to see entirely his own work. Then Papa opened the door, spread his arms, and shouted, 'Now you see.' Inside were hundreds of small statues and ornaments arrayed on shelves, moulded and shaped in plaster of Paris. Beautifully painted with his own hand, they could have been mistaken for works of art. Then, with a sad expression, he confessed, 'I can only sell them on the market stall.' Before we could think of some words to commiserate with him, Mama called us in for tea, the pony giving a neigh of good riddance with our departure.

Such a spread, the laden tea table looked wonderful, everything to delight us, but one in the eye for our pals, who said we would be eating spaghetti, boiled worms their name for it. After tea, we all stayed round the table, and Papa, like his son, talked of Italy. 'We shall buy vineyards, grow grapes and make wine,' he said. Mama nodding and smiling with tears in her eyes, the children chipping in with, 'Us too, Papa.' Looking out of the window at the cold, darkening night, methought, 'Wish they would take me with them.'

Mama, as if reading my thoughts, suddenly jumped up, telling us we should go home before it was dark, and despite our protests that we could find our way home, instructed the roast - chestnut man to see each of us home to our own doorstep. Like Ma, Mama's word was law, and off we went, with our reluctant escort. Many years later, I was to meet again our chestnut friend, an old man now, carbon copy of his Papa, so beloved. Tempted to say, 'you never made it then,' I said nothing, for fear of hurting him.

9

The Procession

Processions through the town were reserved for feast days and Sundays. On this particular Sabbath Day it was the Mayor's 'do'. The sun shone for His Worship, who could placate the gods by leading the marchers into the Parish Church. Barging our way through the sightseers lined up on both sides of the road, we stepped out into the highway, shaded our eyes and gave a running commentary on the processional progress, the police charging after us, and pushing us back into the crowd. Not to be denied, we shouted, 'Here they come,' hurrayed prematurely, and caused onlookers to spill into the cleared thoroughfare, the bobbies straining, shoving and cursing us to eternity.

The Red Cross band was first to appear, making cheerful noises, big drum and euphonium bashing and bumping, the trombones, with far reaching tubes, holding their own, whilst the dulcet tones of clarionet and horn did their utmost to pacify the blast up-front. The band passed by, every man in step, striding out with a peculiar straddle, common to marching bandsmen.

Attention now focused on the Mayor and his cronies, the mace bearer in the lead, garbed like the beadle in 'Oliver Twist', the mace slung over one shoulder, giving him the appearance of a caveman on the rampage. We booed him for no apparent reason, but he was no Scallions and refrained from answering back. Then came the Mayor in splendid isolation, cluttered up and jingling with badges and chains of office, stretched over his ample paunch, and ermine gown, which moved up and down with the rhythm of his tread. We relished the sight of his pompous worship, laughing and booing in turn, whilst the Mayor padded by with a dignity befitting his high office. Aldermen and councillors followed the Mayor, the local undertaker quite relaxed in this sea of affected solemnity. Some had difficulty in keeping up, gasping and sweating in the humid atmosphere. The crowd reacted with dumb insolence, having no time for local politicians.

The crowd shouted, 'It's the Beer and Bacca Band from Little Siberia,' everyone cheered. True or not, the foreigners from Dunstable marched steadily by. Quiet again, the children from a host of Sunday Schools tripped along, girls in galatea hats and starched pinafores, boys unhealthily clean and arrogant, staring at us from the safety of the ranks. We let them pass without comment, knowing they had endured months of regular Sunday School attendance to qualify for this position amongst the august mob.

A posse of police, all six feet tall, stalked by, with the stealthy approach of the night-time bobby catching us unawares, carrying white gloves in the trail position. Those same gloves had reddened our ears on many occasions. Concentrating on the police, we booed and postured like idiots; they in turn making mental notes for our future discomfort.

The boy scouts with rattling side drums and wheezy bugles limped along with extravagant strides. The scoutmaster, grown up and podgy, looking obscene in Baden Powell hat, short knickers and half hose trimmed with ribbons. The young scouts, ardent and loyal, shaming us with their conformity. A platoon of soldiers, arms swinging like railway signals in perpetual motion, came on, wilting when wags in the crowd shouted, 'Saturday night soldiers.' The fire brigade, sporting brass helmets large enough to cover the bandstand, were most impressive, but thigh high boots and heavy serge tunics were making them sweat under the high buttoned-up collars. Peeved at not seeing the fire engine, we jeered and cried, 'Go back and fetch the engine: the Mayor's on fire!'

A massed Salvation Army band went by in silence, presumably having a breather before the next onslaught; the lassies not to be denied, singing lovely hymns to an accompaniment of tambourines, keen eyes under peek-a-boo bonnets egging on young men to be saved.

A few nurses, reeking with starched efficiency, rustled by, a tight little community, out of place with the motley throng, chatting with each other to relieve boredom or embarrassment. The last stragglers, nonentities and makeweights, were out of hearing of the bands, so they put on their own show, flopping about like morris dancers, in an effort to keep in step, mixed up with the milk floats, bicycles, cabs, and all the flotsam following in the wake of the procession spread all over the road. It was time for us to depart, so we scampered off to sanity and what mischief we could find.

10

The Costermongers

The costermongers were a tight-knit clan. Characters like the Hermit, Datetester, Naggy and Maxi, typical of the fraternity. They dressed in exclusive style, suits full cut in check patterns with raised seams, boots hand-made invariably buttoned, and shirts of fine silk.

They could be graded in three sections: the big boys like Stan Parsons and Coulson, who bought in large quantity from Covent Garden and sold at small profit to the lesser men. They had large stalls lit with carbide lamps, selling fruit from a pitch outside the Conservative Club. The second grade stallholders, in position round the Pepper Box, had pitches fronting on to the main thoroughfares, the stalls in vee shape formation compelling would-be customers to operate on two fronts. Lastly came the street hawkers, many of whom having no horse and cart, hired coster barrows for a shilling daily from underneath the Corn Exchange. Not having the capital to buy big variety, they bought single lots, a load of oranges one day and apples the next, hawking them in turn around the town at very competitive prices.

The Market was a jovial place, cries of 'Apple a pound a pear!' 'Kidney Tater!' 'Canary Nana!' echoing round the stalls. Some stalls sold wild rabbits, the costers' cry of, 'Wild rabbit, wild rabbit!' being answered by the crowd, who cried, 'Wrap it

Luton. George Street.

792

George Street with Market Place in foreground and Town Hall in background

up and we'll have it.' All the time costers and customers were exchanging ribald remarks.

At that time a special banana called the Canary Red was on sale in Covent Garden, too dear to sell locally, only high class shops in London having a call for it. A coster called Darbo was delivered a quantity by mistake, but with a philosophy of easy come, he displayed them at normal banana prices. One old dear inspecting the fruit suggested they were not proper bananas, and said he should be locked up for selling such rubbish. It was now Darbo's turn to see red. Digging a gold sovereign from his pocket, he shouted, 'Want to bet on it? Come on lady, let's see the colour of your money.' The old lady declined to wager, but grumbled on, and the fed up coster snatching the hand of bananas off display, peeled one off and wailed, 'I will eat the lot my bloody self!'

On Sunday mornings a number of costers gathered together in Trapps Lane to play Pitch and Toss, Banker and Pitchy up the Mot. This is where we came in as lookouts. Posting ourselves in the hedges at each end of the long lane we watched for the bobbies. Usually they appeared on bikes, fully exposed pedalling along the lane. We had ample time to alert the gamblers, the lookouts spaced out in the hedgerows, relaying the alarm with whistle and hand signal. When the police did arrive little groups of innocent looking strollers hailed them with a polite, 'Good morning, officer.' The frustrated law grunted and pedalled on. Sixpence earned, the police outwitted, made for us a successful Sunday morning.

A donkey given in charity to the costers served them faithfully for many years. The terms of the charity laid down that the animal should be well-treated and never sold. Thus, if a coster becoming affluent had no more use for it, the ass was given to the next deserving case. Terms of the agreement were strictly kept, the donkey prospering with the eagle eye of the fraternity upon it.

With the closure of the open air market and its removal to Plait Hall, most of the atmosphere and gaiety was lost. A new generation of fruit and veg. merchants, with a roof over them, no longer cry, 'Jersey Tater!' and 'Ripe Banana!', content only to wait on customers less choosy with fatter purse. I knew all the old stalwarts, could gossip with them and test the best fruit. Those times have gone, and strolling round the market today, the air of sophistication has the chill of winter about it.

II

Of Cabbages and Kings

'Hi! Hi! Clear the way, here comes the Galloping Major!' A street cry soon muffled when Major Payne looked down on us from his equine height. Togged up in immaculate brown riding boots, with breeches extended to the limit by his ample backside and brown jacket of suede, he looked more like a tailor's dummy than the warrior he was reported to be. A great toper, arrogant, but holding his liquor like a gentleman, we despised his class, and often, to his disgust, ignored him.

We had more respect for Rosie, not to be confused with the Tuppenny Tube, who descended upon our territory like Attila the Hun, with hordes of scruffy urchins from High Town. Products of Gaitskill Terrace and Back Street, their war cry of, 'Coming down your back streets to war, yer,' sent us scuttling off to the safety of home. This amazon, wizened like a pygmy, had a face like leather, spoke with a masculine voice, and was nicknamed Cactus or Leather Lungs. She seemed to have been around for ages, estimates of her age varying from sixteen to sixty.

Bombom (not the schoolteacher) was Jack of all Trades, walker out of cattle from the auction pen, drover, ragman and newsvendor, temporary lamplighter as required, and cleaner-upper after fetes and statties. He tolerated little nonsense from us, running like a deer and never giving up the chase, his hand heavy like lead, descending upon our heads like a poleaxe. His habit of talking to himself led to much mirth, but not when he was within hearing of us.

The skimmed-milk man who was around only on Sundays, hawked skimmed milk at ha'penny a pint, undercutting the regular milkman, who, for fear of prosecution, was forever stirring up the milk's cream content to conform with set standards. The skimmed man had no worries; his horrible liquid did not qualify for the attention of Mr. Peck, the Weights and Measures man. His coster barrow, with the huge churn of milk standing up like the 'Blasted Oak', seemed always to rest outside the pub, the milkman preferring beer to the cream-starved milk he purveyed.

The Curtain King had his pitch on Park Square, an overweight Jew who attracted large crowds of women to his stall by hurling abuse and insults at downtrodden underlings, hired to spread out the yards of material for their inspection. Another crowd puller was the Italian peas seller adjoining the curtain stall. The Jew upbraided the Italian, accusing him of contaminating the beautiful material. 'Take your stinking hot peas away,' he shouted. The Italian, in turn, made rude gestures, telling the Jew to what inaccessible place the rolls of cloth should be stuck.

Ikey Adams was a poacher fat and jovial, with a quick eye for wild rabbits and the odd partridge or pheasant - rumour had it that when game saw him coming it gave itself up. He was expert in the art of bat folding until he lost his nets. Miss Higgins, who kept a bird sanctuary in her spacious garden, caught him bat folding the ivy of her garden wall. Up before another beak he got seven days. The snow and frosts of January were his busiest season, blackbirds, linnets and hedge sparrows in scores becoming victims of his art. Cock linnets and cock blackbirds were sold as song birds. The females and the sparrows sold for sparrow pie. A patch of land bordering on the hedgerow would be baited with bird seed, twin nets stiffened with batons, carefully laid out with two lines fastened to the nets. The lines ran out into the hedge, and another line attached to a braced call-bird did likewise. Ikey, crouching in the hedge, occasionally gave the call-bird a tug. The bird, pegged to the ground, involuntarily fluttered as the line operated and the peg swivelled. Starving flocks of birds, imagining the call was for feeding, swooped down to the scattered seed. Ikey, alert and watchful, pulling on the twin lines, trapped the birds, and extricating the creatures, crammed them in trap cages.

One morning I went with him, the day his luck ran out. Careless placing of his call-bird resulted in the death of his valued enticer. On his first pull, with a hundred linnets in the net area, the nets swung over and the supporting pole landed plum on the captive bird. Ikey, bewailing its untimely end, increased the bird's value each time he sorrowed for its loss.

One night we poached Luton Hoo, armed with extending bamboo pole, noose and lantern. The pole, with the noose attached, yanked down roosting pheasants caught in the lantern beam. A couple of birds in the bag, a hasty exit over the wall into New Mill End Road, across Marslips, through the side streets and home, the pheasants for Ikey, the adventure for me.

The character of Ikey Adams was exposed the morning he took me mushrooming. It was early autumn, hardly light and misty. Entering Poulton's cultivated mushroom fields at Farley Farm, we ran straight into old-man Poulton himself. He manifested from nowhere, his body from the waist down obscured by the low-lying mist. Ikey stood his ground, forbidding me to run, the farmer accusing him of stealing mushrooms. Ikey, with assumed dignity, denied the slander and demanded proof that mushrooms in this field were cultivated. The old man, affronted by such impudence, hurried off to fetch the law. Ikey, who knew the farmer had some distance to go to a telephone, calmly carried on, gathering enough of the edible fungi for a good feed. Then he hustled me away from the field, via Caddington churchyard, Badger Dell, the Lime Kilns, and home.

He scorned notices stating, 'Trespassers will be Prosecuted', even the sign nailed to a tree in Stockwood, saying, 'Beware of Mantraps', and led us in many chestnut bashing expeditions on the estate of the Squire.

Luton in those days was imprisoned by landowners, warning notices everywhere, shutting countryside off from all but the poachers who defied the monopoly of the landed gentry. Squire Crawley's estate stretched along the crest of the hills almost from Luton to Dunstable. The Hoo, with vast acres, was bounded by the New Mill End Road and the A6 barring the east end of the town. North of Luton, Cassels' Putteridge Estate skulked, and beyond Dunstable Woburn, the forbidding Duke of Bedford's domain, not yet plagued by excessive death duties, was an impregnable fortress, guarded by an army of gamekeepers and wardens.

It could be said, with some justification, that Ikey Adams and other poachers were rogues – but offsetting this, the poachers saw, in the selfish hogging of land by gentry, justification for believing they were entitled to share a small part of what came naturally.

12

Growing Pains

'Eat your sausages, are you ill or something?' Saturday night of all nights and left on my plate, three succulent jerks, half buried in fried onions. What matter they would be sour on Monday, the butcher's excuse for his generosity in giving us them. I could not eat them. Usually on this night I could devour a dead horse with the mange. Ma knew this, so she probed for a reason. Finding I had bellyache, her concern subsided and she brewed senna-pod tea. 'To open your bells,' she remarked, 'and drink it whilst it's hot.' Not bad this drink, much better than brimstone and treacle, her recipe for sores.

Our faith in senna pods was misplaced, the ache got worse, so old Gran was called in. 'Could be growing pains, could be,' she said, 'then again he could be putting it on, give him some castor oil, that'll shift it.' Move me it did, to weeping, and I was ashamed of my tears. I hated the old witch, and cried with temper, for this same old Gran had earlier spiked my pawnshop portering job.

No mention of calling in a doctor had been made at this time. Not that I minded, but the ache was beginning to upset me. Doctors were a luxury at half a crown a visit. Besides, in our locality, we knew that doctors went hand in hand with the undertakers. But in the morning, when scrubbed clean, Mother put me in her bed, I realised that the doctor was imminent.

Scared stiff, with head buried under the blankets, I waited for the end.

Ma appeared, pulled the clothes back, told me to mind my manners and ushered the doctor to the bedside. Tall and thin, like a lamp post, elegantly dressed with gold-rimmed spectacles, the medico sported an Albert watch chain across his midriff, the fobs and seals hanging from it, tinkling with each movement he made. Fascinated by the jewellery, I wondered how much Uncle would have loaned on it. 'Where is the pain, laddie?' he asked. I replied, 'All over,' and that was all he gleaned from me.

Prescribing foul tasting medicine, he assured Ma that I had a slight inflammation and some jaundice which would clear up in time. But still I got worse, sweated and swore, dozed on and off, worried about my job, didn't worry about school, and lost interest.

Many half crowns later, Mr. Clarke the butcher came to see me. I asked him about my job, and was assured that it was waiting for me. His knowledge of sick animals stood me in good stead, for he asked Ma to get more expert advice and he would foot the bill. The new doctor found me more co-operative, not that it mattered, for the same day I was wrapped in blankets, carried downstairs and outside to a 'growler'. The cabbie, a jovial old boy smelling of horses and beer, leaned over and shouted, 'Hold on son, we will soon get you to hospital.' His confidence did not comfort me; 'Gran will be laying me out next,' I surmised.

The Bute Hospital, named after the Marquess of Bute, one of the aristocracy who built walls, was a mysterious place adjoining the Workhouse, where it was said that you walked in but were carried out. These things I pondered over, but they carried me in and I would walk out, a philosophy which sustained me in the weeks to come.

Inside, bedded down, screens hid my view of the ward. The mattress, harder than my mother's flock bed, was uncomfortable, but strange too was the soft hot-water bottle. I had been used

The Bute Hospital

to the middle plate of the kitchen range wrapped up in brown paper; this thing at my feet gurgled when I kicked it. Frequent visits of doctors and nurses disturbed my dozes. A nurse painted my stomach, but when she attempted to put white socks on my feet I created merry hell. My protests brought in Ma who I thought had gone home with the cabbie. Her threats of a bashing silenced me, and the dressing-up lark continued, even a white nightgown – one of the nurse's I supposed. When they lifted me on to another bed with wheels on, out into the view of the bedridden patients gawping and crying 'Good luck' into the long corridor, the pace quickened.

I caught a glimpse of Ma sitting bolt upright on a form, dolled up in a russet coloured costume with leg-of-mutton sleeves, suede buttoned boots, and the flat cloth hat trimmed with pheasant's wing feathers, given to her by Lady Talbot. This rig was worn on special occasions like coronations or war victories, so much was it cherished. How many times had Ma worn it? She never bothered with the Boer War when soldiers' wives were adopted by titled ladies. That was years ago, but I felt proud that she wore it for me.

No one up to now had told me what it was all about, so I demanded to know. 'Where are you taking me? What's the matter with me?' These questions the hurrying orderlies ignored until the end of the corridor where the bed with wheels on, and me, were shunted into a small room. Patronising conversation meant for my ears suggested I should be proud to have the same treatment as King Edward. Not everyone was so fortunate. 'Did he get over it?' I asked, trying to rack my brain to remember who was king now, but they gagged me before I could enquire more with an evil-smelling sleep-inducer known as chloroform a rushing sound, a big bang and I knew no more.

Back in bed, my first conscious impression was of my mother sitting by my bedside. She looked worn out in spite of her get-up and I wished they would send her home to bed. I had no time for her; I felt sick, I was too hot and I wanted a drink. No drink was forthcoming and they even tried to stop me being sick. Now Ma was gone, I slept; resolved later to quit this torment and go home. Eventually I did go home – sixteen weeks later.

The time spent in hospital was not uneventful. The peritonitis caused through neglected appendicitis cleared up, and once again, like Muffy Smith's cure of a spiked leg, it would be ungrateful to say I was dead lucky. But the gods were with me, for at a time when anti-biotics had not been dreamed of, even appendicitis without the complications was a deadly ailment.

I had watched, morning and evening, the drainage tubes taken from the open incision in my stomach, washed and returned.

The large black safety pin was carefully fastened to prevent the tube disappearing into the bowel, and I noted with pleasure the tube diminishing in size as the daily painful dressing went on. The final bright day, when the tube was no more and the incision allowed to heal, and I could put my feet on the ground, is the finest moment of my youthful recollection. Now I could use the toilet, no more bedpan stinking to high heaven, no more sticking my penis in the neck of a tin bottle where phlegm still stuck from the spitting of bronchial old men in the ward. I could wallow in baths to my heart's content. No more sensitive young nurses groping around me with blanket baths. I could nose round my fellow inmates, find out what ailed them and compare with my own escape. A new world lay before me and I explored every bed.

Detective Attwood was the most notable one in the ward. In the outside world we avoided him, knowing he meant trouble, but in this sanctuary even he had to tolerate my investigations. I had strong suspicions that it was he who had spat in the bottles, and taxed him with it, but never succeeded in solving the crime.

Come Christmas and a giant tree, presents for all – mine was a book, 'Nat the Naturalist' – and Dr. Bone carving the turkey, my first taste of this bird, so I wished…for more…and got it. Lady Wernher dished out presents. In the evening there were carols and high supper in the Women's Ward. I sat on the bed of Miss Bachini who had St. Vitus Dance, but she didn't dance while I sat there.

Came the New Year and the end of Christmas fare. Back to the main diet of boiled fish, potatoes and rice. But this hospital, depending entirely on charity for its survival, did wonders on its meagre income. Remembering Pound Day and all that soda, I consoled myself with how clean the floors looked.

13

On Music Bent

Came Friday when Doctor, Matron and Sister stood in consultation by my bed, when the doctor told me I could go home tomorrow. That morning I went mad, and dashed round the beds in bare feet and pyjamas bellowing the good news to the ill, the very ill, and the dying, until completely exhausted I was forced back to bed.

On Saturday Ma arrived bringing new clobber, but the ecstasy of yesterday had gone, and I was loath to dress. This place was no mystery now. Loving care and kindness such as I had never known from outsiders before had been inflicted upon me to such an extent, that I dreaded the reality outside those walls. Brusquely, Ma told me to get a move on, but even when ready to depart, I toured the whole hospital again and howled as I said farewell.

Outside, no cab, no emergency either, so we boarded a tram. The rig-out bought for me would have been better suited for a prep. school: short nicks, Norfolk jacket and cap with ear flaps. The conductor, eyeing me up and down, told Ma he thought I looked pale. She countered by asking him if he expected to see a Red Indian. I relaxed, contented; Ma was still the same.

Home to the house, how much smaller it seemed, to the same musty odour of rising dampness and overcrowded habitation, but still clinging to my senses the clinical aroma of ether, the swish of starched uniforms and the reassuring whisper of a nurse at midnight. It was early spring and daffodils in a vase graced the white deal table. 'Did you buy the daffs for me?' I asked Ma, and her embarrassed, 'What made you think that?' told me she had.

This day lasted forever. Ma gabbled on and on, her plans and hopes bursting out from time to time with an eloquence only one of Welsh ancestry could have achieved. I listened spellbound until she told me of her decision to have me taught the piano. Me, to sally forth like Little Lord Fauntleroy, music case and all, in the wake of those cissies, prey to the urchins, who scurried to music lessons, pursued by all of us who frowned upon such stupidity. Not me, and I waxed eloquent in my own cause. 'Get to bed!' cried Ma, without recourse to a threatened bashing. My first night home, I suppose.

Next day, a visit to the doctor, the same one of the Albert chain and tinkling baubles. He recommended a long holiday, special foods to build me up, no violent exercise. Ma told him we would have to get by with no violent exercise. It was at this time that I learned that Mother had the notion I would never be fit for manual work, the heritage of our society; hence my learning the piano.

The piano it was. Two half-hour lessons at a shilling a time from Miss Chapman of Wellington Street, Monday and Friday 5:30 pm to 6:00 pm. Armed with second-hand music case and dog-eared 'Smallwood's Tutor', I was ten minutes late for the first lesson, having skulked down side streets to avoid my fellow urchins. Miss Chapman answered my knock, a small lady, middle aged with a black velvet strap round her neck. Ushering me into the room where the piano stood, she asked, 'Do you know the time?' pointing to her clock. I was about to ask her if her time was right, when she cut me short with, 'You are ten minutes late, which will be deducted from your thirty minutes lesson.'

Even this shortened version seemed endless. Up - the - scale, thumb, first finger, second finger, then thumb and other finger completing the eight notes, right hand, left hand, until finally, 'We will try coming down the scale next lesson. Be sure to practise diligently, and get here on time.'

On my way home I wondered, 'How do I practise diligently without a piano?' Here was a chance to escape from do, re, me, fa, and, to avoid bad luck, I hopped over all the lines on the pavement and prepared to battle with Ma.

'How did you get on? Was Miss Chapman pleased with you? Tell me what you did.'

Hosts of questions until at last I played my ace. 'I can't go any more, we haven't got a piano.'

Ma's feigned surprise fooled me until she blurted out, 'Aunt Emma's giving us her piano.'

Aunt Emma did, and I marked her down. The piano was genuine rosewood, yellow keys, all chipped, the candle holders still containing grease from piano orgies back to Methuselah. The relic looked just fine, like the saloon pianos of westerns, but without bullet holes. Wormholes were there in abundance. So, as always, Ma trumped my ace.

The weekly torment saw progress into *The Bluebells of Scotland* and variations of *Won't You Buy My Pretty Flowers* with pianoforte evenings at home graced by privileged neighbours. Methinks the cheese sandwiches and hot tea were more appreciated than my scales at the piano. I got some consolation by playing the melody with my right hand, with mistakes of course, but thumping on just one chord with the left hand, a kind of left vamping. They never knew, and Ma saw me as the genius of the keyboard.

Miss Chapman wasn't fooled, and threatened to tell my mother that I had no heart for music. Her action was delayed because she found I was very good for fetching her bottled stout from Market Hill. The arrangement continued until Ma, tired of my repertoire, especially the minuet which even I detested, decided her purse was inadequate for the weekly shillings, and broke the news to me that piano lessons had to stop. My delight was overshadowed later by the thought that, had I really tried, the piano and its music were made for me.

14

The Holiday

Although my illness had long been forgotten, Ma's morbid interest in my well-being continued. 'You need a holiday,' she said, 'to put some fat on your bones.'

'To the seaside?' I asked, perking up at the thought of an area I had never seen.

Her reply, 'Where is the money coming from?' quashed the idea; then she outlined her plans for me. It was to be Biscot where a distant relative would board me as a non-paying guest for a few weeks.

Biscot, a small hamlet, four miles from the town, boasted of two farms, Craigs and Hartops, a pond in the road, Parish Church, a nearby school and fifty cottages, mostly owned by the two farmers. Its one landmark was Biscot Mill, looking down on the village from a hill about half a mile distant.

On a fine Sunday we set off to walk the miles to our destination. This was no hardship; I walked longer distances with baskets of meat on most Saturdays. Packed in a brown-paper parcel, tied up with string, the necessities for my holiday were a useful weapon for swatting the insects rash enough to come within range of the swinging parcel. Ma consoled herself that there were no onlookers in the quiet lanes to witness my antics.

Eventually we reached the cottage in Moat Lane, one of a terraced row owned by Mr. Craig the farmer. Inside the cottage,

Biscot Mill

small even by our standards, we were warmly welcomed by a young married couple, the man a farm labourer, the wife a housewife-cum-washer-woman for the site. Here I would enjoy poverty in a rural setting as opposed to poverty in the mean streets of my home.

The cottage, possessing only the bare necessities of roof and walls, could not be termed self-contained. There was no piped water, no gas or electricity, and the toilet was an earth closet thirty yards from the back door. A bath hung on the wall, a

The cottage in Biscot where Aubrey Darby convalesced

large oval contraption, which served for bathing, and as a copper for the mound of soiled linen taken in by the cheerful young woman. The living room, gloomy because of the one small window, contained a deal table, surrounded by hard wheelback chairs. The walls were relieved by two pictures, 'Stag at Bay' and 'The Gleaners'.

The kitchen range always in action, sufficed for cooking, and the boiling up of suds for washing meant that the back door was usually open, ventilation for overheating and steam. The scullery, large enough for two persons with a squeeze, was cluttered with wrinkled apples, firewood and home-made jam. Outside the back door was a communal well, ice cold, but always flecked with little black smuts. It was said the well failed but once, when a dead cat emerged in a bucket. The stairs to the bedrooms were almost perpendicular, abysmal darkness making the ascent more hazardous.

Away from this hutch of habitation a new world opened up: the pond in the lane where horses and ducks shared with me the joy of cool contact with the tadpole-infested water, the Old Moat Farm, thatched and ancient, the jovial farm hands, and the meandering brook skirting the lane and losing itself in the water meadows below Hartop's farm. The Mill was forever turning. There was the wealth of aquatic life in the marshes beyond the meadows, watercress for the picking, and the thrill of paddling in reeds and finding duck's eggs. I walked this wonderland alone, selfish in the thought that no living person shared it with me, until one day I came upon three village boys.

'Hey, town boy, go back to where you come from,' they shouted, and I was back to reality.

'Clodhoppers, Mangel Wurzels,' I shouted back, and walked towards them. They stood their ground, and we eyed each other, and said no more.

Then one boy queried, 'On holidays hereabouts are you?' Still I passed on without comment, abashed, and one lad remarked, 'Funny lad, ain't he?' The incident forgotten, I sauntered on, enjoying every detail of country life, but excited with everything the village boys thought commonplace.

There were no shops in the village, but the young housewife, expert at making toffee, supplied me with sweets. The toffee, with a hint of vinegar, was delicious. Her cooking too was marvellous, a plentiful supply of milk, carried home a gallon at a time by her husband, ensuring milk puddings galore. Eggs were always on the table, two whole eggs, a feast compared with the shared egg of more frugal days. The odd pheasant also graced the table, nit putrid with hanging, but fresh caught, with mum's the word if anyone asked. Rabbit served as pie, stewed or baked, never tasted so good, even chicken to gladden the Sabbath day. This was not rural poverty, it was rural paradise, and I waxed strong, whistled, sang and jigged in the lanes.

The last treat of my holiday was the trip into Luton on a pig float, the man of the cottage having been instructed to pick up farm implements from the railway goods-siding. Perched precariously on a plank stretched across the float, we jogged into town. The huge plough horse's ears pricked, plodding along, disdainfully eyeing the seedy town horses as we threaded our way through the traffic.

Having loaded the float, the bit was removed from the animal, a nose-bag of food hung over the horse's head, and we sat down on the siding platform and fed on hard-boiled eggs, cheese and bread, all the while dangling our legs over the platform edge. Cold tea washed down the repast, then we made tracks for home. A stop at the water trough, and the horse drank his fill, up the hill, past the winding sails of the mill, a long trek down the lane, and the village came in sight, man and boy silent, but both anticipating the evening meal.

The meal was, as usual, up to expectation, and afterwards the subject of my return home came up. 'Your mother is coming for you on Sunday, but you can stay longer if you want to,' the young woman told me. Tempering her generosity with an expression of my mother's, that I didn't want to wear out my welcome, I suggested it would be nice to stay longer, but the last word would be with Ma.

On the Sunday Ma arrived, soaked to the skin, for it had rained heavily all morning. Made comfortable, dried out and fed, she listened to my pleas to stay on, heard my host's assurance of extended welcome, but plainly stated I must come home, for my holiday was over. On the way home she nattered on how well I looked, promising I could go back next year. To all her chatter I kept silent, then she blurted out, 'I wanted you home, the place is a graveyard with you away!' Now I understood, and felt peeved with my own thoughtlessness. Grabbing her arm, I returned the compliment, the holiday forgotten in this latest get-together.

Today, Biscot is no longer a rural paradise. It is a built up area, and part of Luton. The lanes are now metalled roads, the windmill gone, and what was the water meadows is now an estate of semi detached houses, monotonous and typical of modern planning. The pond has gone and the little brook no longer meanders, but is captured in a series of culverts of sewer-like persuasions. The Old Moat Farm House still stands, not as the warm centre of a farming community, but miraculously brought back to resemblance of its ancient history as an inn. The old farm wagon in the car park rebukes the masquerade, looking down with disgust on the pseudo moat, its water contained in sheets of polythene.

The cottage in Moat Lane is still there, so is the apple tree, sterile now, but still alive. In the garden beside that tree, I glimpsed the rolling uplands, the distant windmill, and cloud shadow speeding over the waving cornfields.

The Church, unchanging, stands for eternity, and the headstones mark the waiting dead; the school adjoining is closed and silent like the graves. Has anyone pondered what they had in mind – the ancients who plotted playground and graveyard side by side? Yet hailstones engraved in stone, 'which fell as big as this', are preserved for posterity in the bar of a resurrected Moat Farm-cum-inn.

15

Diddle Smith

After the months in hospital and the musical interlude, during which time I had cut myself off from society, I made friends with Diddle Smith. Diddle, one of a family of fifteen children, lived in Buxton Road, right opposite the school entrance. This gave him stature in my eyes and our friendship deepened. Diddle's father was a bookmaker's runner, a job with adventure, concerned mainly in dodging the police who frowned upon street betting and three-pence-each-way backers, bent on getting rich quick. Diddle and I helped outwit the law by collecting betting slips handed us by runners who generally lurked in pub lavatories at mid-day opening times. The betting slips, some on fag packets, some on newspaper margins, none on toilet rolls - presumably these had not been invented - were rushed off to the bookmaker who lived in the residential area. This is where Diddle and I excelled, running about half a mile to the big house and handing the parcel in before the first race. From our observations Diddle and myself were the only ones in the profession who ran.

All of Diddle's brothers and sisters had nicknames, Dodger, Lardie, Greasy and so on. They soon gave me one – Dabby, which with slight variation has lived with me for sixty years. It was a proud family and I told myself I was one of them. Seventeen in all, living in a two bedroomed terraced home: an attic, two living rooms and a cellar, where every Thursday I joined them in a hot chitterling supper. There was one toilet outside, thirty yards from the back door, and no bathroom.

Bath night on Fridays lasted for hours, each in turn, bathing in hot water from the copper in the cellar. The weekly ablutions were timed like a military operation, and woe betide anyone of the family being late for parade.

At school Diddle and I were inseparable. Any boy wanting to fight had to fight both of us, so we prospered and knew it would never end. This pal of mine, just ordinary, dark untidy hair, with dark brown eyes, small for his age, possessed a wonderful singing voice, so rich in tone that when we were singing his voice could be heard beyond us all. The teachers knew this but could never persuade him to sing solo or accept voice training, so like many of our class and generation, talent was allowed to decay.

The frequent tragedy of young babies dying with enteritis struck down Diddle's two-year-old twin brothers, and he accepted my mother's invitation to stay with us at weekends. The extra titbits she stored up for us made life much more abundant.

Springtime, and Diddle's amazing eye for finding birds' nests: the joy in feeling warm eggs as stretched hands felt into the nest tempered with his, 'Only take one, then there will be more next year,' endeared me more and more to him. In his own way he taught me that philosophy was based on logic. In the summer we pitched our home-made sacking tent on Spike Island, waking up at first light covered in dew and cow dung through rolling down the hillock in our sleep. We adventured into poultry farming when we snaffled a broody hen. To our delight, and the consternation of wellwishers, ten chicks hatched out.

There were halcyon days, and the dog days when we bought a mongrel puppy off Scallions for sixpence. We trained it in our fashion, expecting the animal to catch hares and rabbits. Small head, big feet, long-haired with sorrowful eyes, all the dog caught was fleas, but we loved it. This lovable hound, we called Gyp, accepted two masters and favoured neither of us. A happy relationship lasted two years, when the hound died with distemper. What religion we had died with its passing.

16

Coming Out

The summer of 1911 was hot, with frequent thunderstorms. George V was crowned, later to be followed by his son's ennobling as Prince of Wales. To celebrate the occasion, we marched in procession to Luton Hoo, decked out in the uniform of some particular part of the far-flung empire. The long walk was tiring, and keeping in tune with the band, almost out of hearing, developed into a hop, skip and jump, as we were commanded to keep step. Nevertheless, we felt more charitable to the new monarch when scoffing heaps of bread and jam, cakes and lemonade, sacrificed before us in the lush meadows of the aristocrats. Horseflies, bumblebees and wasps also rose to the occasion, and we sang, 'God save the King,' with a new fervour. Dignitaries moved among us, deigning to accept the offered bun with grace and dignity. Bone china coronation mugs, with King and Queen painted on, were caressed by children and guarded as though they were gold. Such vessels would never hold cocoa, doomed forever to adorn shelves and overmantles, stuffed with pins and pawn tickets.

Back to school, and for penance, write a composition on the coronation and what it meant to us. One boy wrote, 'Queen Victoria did not come because she was dead.' Another stated in all truth, 'The best part we liked was the tea in the Hoo,' statements giving much anger to Bom Bom our teacher. One bright boy's

epistle was read to the class; this literary masterpiece fooled the
teacher but not us, we knew his capabilities. My effort was not
commented upon, praise enough for 'Uneasy lies the head'.

Soon after this, a boy I had never associated with invited me
to his birthday party. I accepted after making certain he was not
joking. I could not recall ever doing him a favour, or giving him
any treasure, but my mother's, 'He is such a nice refined boy,' set
my doubts at rest. Taking the invite very seriously, Ma saw to it
that I was neat and tidy for the party. White blouse and celluloid
collar, new braces to hoist up my oversize knickerbockers, and
off I went with Mother's, 'Make sure you say please and thank
you very much,' ringing in my ears.

The boy's mother answered the door to my knock, smiling
benevolently, but behind her a sea of faces stared at me,
hostile and curious. Introductions all round failed to allay my
misgivings, for among the crowd were cissies whom my own
crowd had baited in the past. Before tea we played games: Pass
the Parcel, Musical Chairs, and so on. At this time my neck
began to rebel at the unaccustomed stiff collar, and I perspired
freely. The hoisted-up knickerbockers cut into my privates, and
I knew then it was a mistake to come.

The tea cheered me up. Such a spread, they must have been
rich! Tomatoes, cucumber, the lot, and a birthday cake bigger
than Ma's flat hat. We toasted the boy on his birthday, not
in sherbet water, but proper lemonade. Then the bashful lad
proceeded to open his birthday presents. Opening each parcel
in turn and expressing delight at the contents, he thanked the
donors interrupted by his mother's remarks: 'How thoughtful,'
'Really you shouldn't have,' 'Lucky boy,' and so on. Asked by
some nosy guest what I had given, my reply, 'Nowt with knobs
on,' so puzzled him that we had moved on to more games before
he could work it out.

Then to wind up the evening, the lady announced we would
all circle the table for Snap Dragon. This was new to me, and I

watched her place a large bowl in the middle of the table, fill it with dried fruit, and over the whole lot pour brandy. Then she plunged the room in darkness and set light to the bowl. With squeals of delight, tentative fingers made passes at the bowl, extracting the odd raisin. Believing this to be a test of daring-do, and a chance at last to come into my own, in I dived with both hands, scooping up the whole contents of the bowl. The squeals turned to murmurs, then into silence, and the room, now lit-up, revealed my two fistfuls of flickering raisins. Realising my mistake, the fruit returned to the bowl, and I hoped they would laugh at my expense. There was no laughter, only an aloofness that hurt. I left the gloom and sauntered home, chafing collar, sore crutch, and no present to give, forgotten in this last humiliation. I told Ma how I enjoyed the party; there was no joy in making her miserable too.

17

If Winter Comes

It was the end of March, spring was in the air and already Mother, impatient for Garden Beautiful, had sown a packet of flower seeds in the two foot square of earth made available by removing a flag stone in the yard. March was going out like a lamb, soon the fire would not need stirring.

On this particular afternoon the sun shone and the class was reciting, 'While the chaffinch sings on the orchard bough,' - (thought I, 'Not if Ikey Adams spots it,') – 'in England now.' Suddenly the sun went in, and it was cold. The classroom fire, usually hidden by Bom-Bom's posterior, was low in the grate, and outside a few snowflakes frolicked in the gusting wind.

Coming home from school, the sudden darkness had caught the lamp lighter unawares, an atmosphere of sadness enveloping us in the gloom. Inside, a poke at the damped-down fire brought flame and light to cheer the room, and while waiting for Ma, the wind, having become a mournful howl, seemed to be descending the chimney of the firelit room, and outside the snow, in horizontal deluge, blanketed the ground. At ease again, when Ma came home all covered in snow, my query as to whether the butcher would want me that night was answered by, 'You must go and find out – bring home a fourpennyworth of neck o' mutton, and ask him to throw in a bit of suet.' Stew was in the offing later on, and well worth waiting for.

Outside the blizzard raged, blowing me up the alley. It was as cold as Christmas, but in the shop a considerable warmth from my boss, who told me to hurry back home, because only dogs ventured abroad on a night like this. Clutching the newspaper – wrapped mutton, I made for home, but when I ran into the alley, the gale blew me off my feet. Scrambling up again, and leaning into the wind, progress was made, with occasional turning my back to the elements in order to breathe again, I arrived home. Mother greeted me with, 'What's happened to the meat?' Calamity. I had forgotten to pick it up when I fell over. Saying no more but slaying me with a look, Ma shawled up and went forth, returning later empty handed. One of the dogs spoken of by the butcher must have scoffed it, but I dared not suggest that to Ma.

All night long the blizzard raged, the falling whiteness congealing into drifts of mountainous heights. Crashing telegraph poles went down unheard, the awful wind having monopoly of sound. In the morning, snow in undulating curves transformed the bleak alley into a magic scene. No school today, the excuse plain to see, so we would scrounge broom and shovel, call upon the elite and shift the beautiful snow for a modicum. Downs Road, the abode of the privileged, venue for horse-dung, flogging and Christmas carolling, this was our destination, and they were pleased to see us.

Ten bob a piece we earned that day, plus a bonus I got from Mrs. Dryden when her Pekinese dog bit my finger. A cup of tea, a lump of cake, and concern over my slight injury, amply compensated for a finger already painless from the cold.

That evening I dared to mention the scarpered mutton, wealth from snow heaving giving me great confidence. 'It's an ill wind,' said Ma, poking away at the fire, from the top of which the smell of stew and little dumplings wafted from an agitated saucepan lid. Recalling the winters of my boyhood, they seemed much more severe in those days, but they were enjoyable. We made slides on the sloping paths of Dallow Road Rec., becoming experts in Littleman, Zig Zag and One Leg, hurtling down the polished ice at frightening speed with the grace of ballet dancers. I never owned a real sledge, just a piece of corrugated iron. This I cherished, being able to bend and shape it to suit particular slopes. Winter warmers, made from cocoa tins, were essential winter gadgets. The tin, with small holes punched in it, was filled with smouldering rag and whirled around by a wire threaded through the holes, the tin glowing red hot with the draught.

The stars blinked alive in the winter night, solitaires of blue ice, and clusters of sparkling diamonds. On clear, cold nights, with frost on the slates, we gazed at the stars, pointing out the Plough, the Bear and the distant planets. We debated at length, could this be the floor of heaven? Could the stars be holes in the floor? We gave up and twirled the winter warmers once more. No mystery here, they were our own creation. We were more positive when we saw a shooting star that someone, somewhere, was having a baby.

18

Beside the Seaside

Diddle and I became friendly with Arthur Thomas through our business connections, flogging him horse dung at twopence a boxful. Arthur, who worked in the hat trade, was a keen gardener, who performed miracles with an allotment beyond Spike Island, despite his plot of land having a one in three slope, being chalky and plagued with wireworm, bindweed and slugs. The horse dung, rich and free from straw, played no mean part in the allotment's yield, Arthur acknowledging our part in his success. He was a keen follower of the Sport of Kings, our connections with bookmakers again of assistance to him with the placing of wagers. So it came about that he invited us to spend three days with him at Brighton, where we could enjoy the sea, and he could make his fortune on the racecourse. Besides paying our expenses he would give us pocket money, the one stipulation that permission be obtained from our parents. After a word with our friend the two mothers were satisfied that everything was above board, and we awaited the day.

On the August Tuesday, there being no racing on the Monday, we set off, the necessities of my holiday, shirt, Sunlight soap and towel neatly tied in a brown paper parcel. Diddle, swanky like, sported a cardboard attaché case purchased from the sixpenny bazaar at great expense. Catching the 6:30 a.m. workmen's train from Luton, we grabbed window seats and enjoyed every minute of the passing countryside as the grimy train rattled towards London. Arriving at the metropolis we hurried along St. Pancras platforms, aware of the great steam engines and the echoing sounds of the terminus. Along the subway to the tube, and we had two changes of trains before reaching Victoria Station. All this time Arthur clutched the morning paper, scanning the racing columns at every available moment. Tickets for Brighton bought, Arthur led us into the buffet and bought three cups of tea, sat down and fished out a bagful of brawn sandwiches. These we scoffed before our benefactor settled on his choice of nags, stuffed the paper into his jacket pocket, and rushed us off to the excursion train bound for the coast. The journey down was uncomfortable, single compartments with no toilets, presumably the outcome of cheap excursion tickets. The compartment was crowded, a posse of small kids commandeering the window seats, obscuring the view outside, and climbing all over us.

Arrived at Brighton, we hurried down the hill towards the sea. Arthur was anxious to get us settled before he went to the races. 'There's the sea,' he told us, looking ahead.

'Where?' we shouted, for all we could see was the sky.

'In front of you,' he grumbled. So it was, and we, who had never seen it before, mistook the sea for sky. A quick look at the ocean and we were off again, digs not yet found and only an hour left before the first race.

In a back street, not unlike our own street, we found lodgings, bed and breakfast, three shillings a night, sleeping three in a bed, a chamber pot, plain white, serving as lavatory. The bedroom in the basement was lit by gas; on the floor a tatty rug hid faded oilcloth and, apart from this, no other luxuries.

Our friend, noting the time, gave us half-a-crown apiece, fixed a rendezvous outside The Ship, and was off. We would find the sea and start holiday making. Scrambling over the endless pebbles, we pulled up short at the water's edge, fascinated by the perpetual motion, tugged off boots and stockings, and waded in.

We were not alone – women with ample skirts tucked in fleecy bloomers, and men showing their braces, strutted about with trousers rolled up to the knees. Children in rompers squealed with excitement, and the odd demure bathing costume of the upper class was mixed up with the rabble. Tired of splashing around, we left the frolics and made for the pier: half dollars were made for spending.

On the pier we squandered a tanner before realising the slot machines were a swindle. No matter how we banged and rocked the contraptions, no prize came out. So we bought rock, liquorice and lemonade, gazed out at the mighty ocean, and kidded each other it was heaven. Forsaking the uncomfortable pier seats, we tramped off to meet Arthur, standing outside The Ship Hotel for what seemed years until he arrived. With expectation of a meal to come, he led us round until we came to a windowful of good grub: sausages, onions, tomatoes, every conceivable delicacy was frying before our hungry eyes. Dashing in, we sat down on high backed benches arranged in cubicles, ordered sausages and fried onions, bread and tea, sat back and awaited the repast. The food tasted as good as it smelt, and our benefactor, pleasantly surprised by the economics of the bill, suggested we have another cup of tea and a little cake. Now we were enjoying the holiday, full up and rested, we looked forward to the rest of the evening.

The night life of Brighton was not for us, a breeze coming off the sea chilled us, and Arthur, insisting on squatting in the lee of the wind, was content to sit and natter about racing and gardening. A last look at the oily swell swilling under the pier stanchions, and we made tracks for the doss house. Sleep came quickly, for the sea air had tired us out, and we awoke the next morning to grumbling Arthur, complaining we took up all the bed. A bowl of cold water, part of the service, sufficed for our ablutions, a walk up two flights of stairs, and we sat down to streaky bacon and fried plum tomatoes. Chunks of bread cut like doorsteps were enough to soak up all the tomato juice. The tea, like the proverbial cat's water, was unlimited in supply.

This was to be our last day at the seaside, for on the morrow we were to be off very early for the journey home. Once more, Arthur was off to the races, but consoled us with pocket money of five bob each, reminding us that we should take presents home to our parents. The rest of that morning was spent in choosing gifts to take home. I settled for a piece of Goss, emblazoned with Brighton coat of arms. It was very expensive, knocking my pocket money for two bob. Diddle went for quantity, a dozen sticks of rock for two bob. Fair's fair, we both squandered the same amount, and scampered down to the beach. This second encounter with the sea was an anti climax; we paddled, saw the same bloomers and braces, scoffed rock, and forsaking the pier, wandered along the front. Pubs, eating houses and stall holders flanked our stroll, the monotonous in and out sea nothing like our imagination pictured it. I would be glad to be home, and felt homesick for my back alley and the green hills beyond.

19

The Games

Sixty years ago neither wireless nor television had intruded into family life. Most people retired to bed before nine p.m., lighting was by gas or oil lamp, and in winter time the large, open coal fire was an added source of light. Indoor games were enjoyed, draughts and dominoes being the most popular. Ludo, snakes and ladders and snap were very popular with the younger children. Games of twopence halfpenny, ha'penny brag and whist were played by adults, who gambled for coppers. Usually when the adults gambled the children were sent to bed.

Supper, about 7.30 pm, was provided in every home – onion gruel, a mixture of boiled onions and flour seasoned with pepper, salt and vinegar – cheese and Spanish onion – chitterlings, home-made faggots with pease pudding – pigs' tails and trotters, and many more economical dishes, tasty and cooked to perfection by careful housewives.

The average family of the poorer class consisted of mother and five children, so when the boys were about ten years of age and working evenings and Saturdays, they tended to forsake the home and find amusement in street games. Band of Hope, a young temperance movement, appealed only for obtaining enough stars to qualify for the outing each year. Public houses were patronised for the empty bottles we pinched from the back, and swapped for pennies at the front.

Lamp posts and walls had to be climbed. The former, either to turn out the gas mantle or swing from the ladder bracket just under the lantern. The latter, just because the wall was there, or in the case of the formidable workhouse wall which ran along one side of Dallow Road rec. to sample the luscious apples in September.

Telegraph poles were a challenge, but after climbing the first ten feet iron footholds made the remaining height very easy to climb. Free-riding the back of drays, coal carts and timber wagons was a hazard, for when passers-by shouted, 'Whip behind, Mister,' the whip lash often scourged us before we could jump off. Riding the axle of the tall agricultural carts was more hazardous still, but out of reach of the whip we could thumb a nose at the 'whip behind' merchants.

Hoop trundling was a seasonable past time, the boys rolling iron hoops with skidder attachments, the girls with wooden hoops and sticks. After the hoops came top flogging. Carrot, turnip and mushroom tops with silver paper and coloured chalk prettied up as the top revolved. The mushroom top, beloved of boys, soared into the air when clanged correctly, and if no wall or window hindered flight the top landed yards away and still continued to spin. Five stones, marbles and fag-card flicking all followed in strict rotation, but with the autumn nights group games began, interrupted only by bonfire night and carol singing. Back alleys, stables and communal back yards were back cloths to the games, the street lights the stage lighting. Truss, catty, hounds and hares, the parcel game, tappet, squat, knights and captains and kick-tin games for the boys. Statues, all this side of the window's mine, I- spy and nurses, were games strictly for the girls.

Hound and hares, a game in which any number of boys took part, depended for its success on the courage and fleetness of the boy chosen to be the hare. Given five minutes start, the hare restricted to a block of streets, was allowed to go anywhere within the limits, be it house, pub, backyard, shop, stable or slaughter house. The hounds followed the hare wherever he went, the game ending when he was cornered and tapped on head and backside. Very often, twenty boys would chase the hare, the pursuers chasing it over walls and fences, even through public house bars. On one occasion the hare took refuge in a Band of Hope meeting. The speaker was left speechless by so many scruffy converts suddenly entering the hall. When the hare walked out, most of the hounds stayed behind, the eye of the pastor forbidding more departures.

The parcel game, in which a neatly tied parcel was placed on the pavement convenient to a passage or alleyway, with a long string attached to it, gave much amusement. Any passerby seeing the parcel would pause, look around and then stoop to grab the prize. With the parcel almost at hand, a jerk on the string, and the parcel flew down the passageway. We always chose an alleyway with an escape route, although the victim rarely came in pursuit. But on the night an old lady reported to the police that a cat in a box was running about in the street, we had a visit from the local constable warning us to pack the game up.

Catty, a game played with two long sticks and a short piece of wood pointed at both ends, was a crude game of cricket. Two rings, eight paces apart, were chalked on the pavement, each ring one pace in diameter. The short stick, the catty, was aimed at the ring and the batsman at that end tried to hit the catty. If succceding, the batsman ran between the rings, scoring runs until the catty was retrieved. If the striker missed, and the catty fell into the ring, he was out, but if the catty fell outside the ring then the batsman was allowed three tries at tipping the catty into the air and swiping it. The pointed ends of the short stick when tapped, caused the catty to jump off the ground, and the boys became very skilled in the reflex action of tapping and hitting, so did the fielder in catching the small piece of wood as it sped an eccentric course through the air.

Truss was a game similar to leap frog. One boy, his back to a wall, acted as cushion. Two sides each comprising of about ten boys contested the game, one side made a back bending down in a long line, the first one in the line with his head cushioned in the stomach of the lad standing at the wall. The other side then leaped on to the line of bent backs. The best jumpers went first to give more room for the others. When all were on, and if the line had not collapsed under the weight, then the other side had their turn. Tragedy finally marred this game when one boy suffered permanent injury to his spine.

Tip up those golden balls was a game rarely played, as there was little credit in it. The unfortunate boy who became judge was usually a newcomer to the street or of simple mind. The game consisted of judge, gaolers and convicts. The judge, who felt honoured in being chosen, sat on a doorstep, and the convicts were marched out of his sight to bring back the golden balls stolen by them out of the judge's view. They collected rubbish of all kinds, including horse manure, and then marched back to be sentenced by his lordship. After being lined up in front of the judge, he commanded them to 'tip up the golden balls,' whereupon they pelted him with the collected rubbish. Irate housewives, opening the front door to see what was going on, invariably received their share of the loot, and the poor judge, cowering from the shower, was kicked off the doorstep.

Kick-tin, squat and release were all forms of hide and seek. Knights and captains consisted of two sides, each boy carrying a piece of paper with his rank written on it. One boy only had a captain's paper. If he was caught the rest had to surrender, so the artful dodgers had numerous rules to prevent his capture.

Tap it and Knock up Ginger were games indulged in for tormenting households. Knock up Ginger was simply bashing on a door and running like hell. Tap it, a more sophisticated torment, needed a small button, a length of black cotton and a pin. The button, suspended by the cotton over a window, swung like a pendulum with the slightest wind, and made a tapping noise on the window pane. The occupants, puzzled by the tapping, made frequent visits to the front door, but in the darkness rarely found the cause of the irritating tapping.

Every home had a pin cushion. Mainly heart-shaped, the cushions were made up of brightly coloured velvet, edged with beads and filled with sawdust. The more daring women made pin cushions in the shape of prima donnas' large bosoms, using great skill in reproducing the desired effect. Boys saw only the pins sticking out, took them and lay them on the tramlines. When the tram passed over them, according to how the pins were placed, miniature swords, daggers, letters of the alphabet, and numbers were fashioned.

The large back door keys of the old morticed locks came into great demand when one boy filled the hollow shaft of a key with match heads, placed a nail in the open end, and then knocked the nail in by bashing it against a wall. The resulting explosion delighted us, but missing keys put a stop to our new-found game.

Most habitations, warehouses and shops had basements, or as we called them, cellars. Gratings covered the area below ground, but let daylight into the below-ground windows. The iron gratings were fixtures, so if anything of value fell through the grating, it could only be retrieved by the owner of the property. This led to boys enjoying another past time. Equipped with a piece of soap, always Sunlight, and a long stick, it was eyes down at every grating. When anything of value was seen, the soap was fixed on the end of the stick. The stick pressed down on the object and the prize extracted. Ha'pennies and pennies were frequently found; the only silver found was a little tizzy or threepenny piece.

August 1914 changed everything. The young men marched off to fight for freedom and the urchins grew up overnight. Three days at school, three days filling in the gaps left by the men, and on Sunday, digging up any spare land and planting spuds, left no time for the games. The slogan, 'Your King and Country needs You!' weighed heavily on the conscience.

We wore putties, sported cap badges of every battalion in sight, and ran errands for troops billeted in the schools once thought necessary for our education. We read the stop press bulletins, brought up to date from the papers printed the day before, and understood at last the meaning of 'more casualties'.

Although the fighting was overseas, telegraph boys brought home to us the carnage in those far off fields. Had we played Knock up Ginger or Tip those Golden Balls, we would have tramped on the unknown graves of those who opted out. These days a pulse was beating in the minds of youth. We grew up in the grim days, but the interrupted games of our childhood left a legacy of stunted growth and starved education. Mothers watched their sons grow up, and prayed for an end to war before the offspring aged sufficiently to march away. The boys were itching to go, and many a fifteen-year-old 'man' wangled his way into khaki. God was on our side, we knew that, so we listened to the prophets in the market place on Sunday night, and did not scoff when they warned us, 'This is Armageddon.' But why all the young men had to be slaughtered before the millennium came, was beyond our simple reasoning. What a game everyone played, and at the end the promised rainbow, but for a million souls that pledge was not redeemed.

20

Rough Justice

The bailiff, or bum, was a character feared by most of the struggling community. Armed with a restraining order, he could enter the abode of the debtor and live in the home for three days and three nights. At the end of this period the auctioneer sold sufficient chattels to cover the debt and the cost involved. It was not unusual for everything to be sold, because the pitiful furnishings had little value. The bum was a man of big build, thick-skinned, incorruptible, but there was one occasion in our street when the bum was outwitted.

This particular bum, known for his liking for ale, was regaled by the household with beer laced with whisky, and encouraged to sleep off the effects. During his sleep, everything except the bed he lay on was spirited away by helpful neighbours. Little could be done in law to recover the property. The debtor, with no apparent assets, could only be sent to gaol for pilfering his own goods. To the desperate this was no hardship; they were assured of food and lodging for a time.

Juvenile offenders met with little sympathy from the magistrates. The birch and reformatory schools were accepted punishments for the most trivial offences. I was a hostile witness in court when one of my fellow urchins was awarded five strokes of the birch. It was during the school holidays, we were camping out under sacking tents on the hills overlooking some gardens. A boy who was camping with us espied some large green cooking apples on a tree in one of the gardens, and suggested we scrump a few.

Knowing the owner of the fruit as a wily old bird, and aware of our presence in the vicinity, we tried to dissuade the lad from pinching the apples. We were all hungry at the time, the cindered spuds roasted in our wood fire having filled us up with wind, leaving our stomachs with large cavities. Still we refused to go, so the boy went alone and was caught in the act. Though it was nearly midnight the crafty old man sensed his apples would be raided and lay in wait.

A fortnight later our pal appeared before the magistrates. On the clerk's table three golden apples reposed in a basin, damning evidence against our camp mate. Having been called as witnesses, we, the other three campers, had to attend court, but when a policeman held up the apples for the magistrates to see, we started to giggle, were admonished from the bench and told we should be treated as hostile witnesses. The proceedings dragged on, and Old Wily Bird told the court we were always stealing his fruit. The accused truthfully told the beak it was the first time he had pinched anything, and we were warned to keep from bad company. Telling the boy he was to receive five strokes of the birch, the magistrate warned that this time he was being lenient, but come before him again and he would go to reformatory school. This mate of ours took his punishment, and even suggested next day that having been birched for the apples we should go to the police station and ask for them back.

How far have we advanced today from birching young boys to suspended sentences for criminal offences? From caning children, incapable of learning, to three months' gaol for beating babies to a pulp, from reformatory school for playing truant to pandering of students who commandeer colleges, stage sit-ins and wreck buildings. Have we progressed? Someone else must answer: I am old with discontent.

Justice in school was symbolised by the cane. The long slender persuader, hanging from the easel, a constant visual threat. On this particular morning, a scholar not endowed with much intelligence or endeavour took the headmaster's eye. Partitions and curtains dividing the classes were pulled back, and the boy made to stand on the master's desk. 'Gaze upon this wretch!' cried the head, 'here you see an example of laziness personified, a lout with no backbone or spunk!' The word spunk was a term used in a different sense to the head's interpretation. Consequently, we all began to smirk. He immediately saw the reason for the mirth, lined us up in single file, and caned the whole school. Then, exhausted, he retired from the assembly, leaving the spunkless boy still standing on the desk, grinning like a Cheshire cat. In our eyes, justice had not been done, but the culprit had a bird's eye view of our discomforture. Possibly in his eyes, justice must have been seen to be done.

'Be prepared', the watchword of the Boy Scouts, should have prepared me for its disciplined justice. Having joined up mainly with the annual camp in mind, the eagerly awaited Saturday morning muster arrived. An essential part of the kit was two blankets to be provided by the boys' parents. Ma had two spare blankets stored away, best white witneys, reserved for illness and unexpected visitors. Knowing it was useless to ask for them, I took them while her back was turned, and dashed off to the group. With the blankets safely packed on the hand cart, the column paraded and prepared to march off to Totternhoe, a village six miles distant. Suddenly down the hill came Ma, shouting, 'Stop! Stop!' waving her arms. 'Where are they?' she gasped.

'On the hand cart,' said I, and without more ado, she threw bundles in all directions before grabbing her precious witneys. Then, clouting me on the ears, she marched off, leaving me to face the laughing scouts.

Called to order by the scout leader the laughter ceased, and I was offered blankets by the leader. Stunned by the humiliation, I refused the offer and ran off, sulked in the alley and decided that I never wanted to camp anyway. Reasoned I, was Ma wrong? But loyalty forbade me to suggest that she was wrong. The final scout episode came later in the year. The scout hut was in a loft, lighting was by gas, and the gas meter was placed under the stairs. Varied japes were played from time to time. One lark was turning off the gas at the meter and leaving the loft in darkness. Warnings of dire punishment had little effect, and one night I crept up to the meter and turned it off. Sure enough, on this occasion they lay in wait, and I was caught, court martialled and slung out. The fact that I had helped to finance the purchase of one cymbal counted for nothing. Other boys had turned off the gas; my crime was in being caught.

Rough Music, justice meted out by neighbour upon neighbour, was an odious carry-on. With rows of terraced hovels, communal back yards and privies, everything that happened quickly spread around. Having the bums in, and drunkenness, were accepted as part of life, but whoring brought down the wrath of the community upon the transgressor. Having proved guilt by hearsay and gossip, the neighbours gathered together, and equipped with music makers made up of dustbin lids, tin cans, rattles and toy drums, paraded outside the home of the alleged whore, and commenced to rough music the household. The din was earsplitting, and the occupants, with no light showing, cowered away from the vigilantes. Strangely, the bobby on the beat was always missing on these musical occasions, and the victims were too scared to come out in protest. Next day the alleged whore and her family moved out, knowing that by staying they invited another night of terror.

I witnessed two sessions of rough music as a young boy, and in each case the crowd whipped themselves up into a frenzy of hate. Now, as an old man with two world-wars under my belt, there seems to be no difference between that back-street justice and the organised brutality of so-called civilised nations.

21

The Labour Exam

The school notice-board rarely attracted our attention, unless we wanted a drawing pin for some notorious purpose, but this Monday morning it caused much excitement. Read the notice:-

BOYS OF TWELVE YEARS WHO HAVE REACHED THE SEVENTH STANDARD OF EDUCATION ARE ELIGIBLE TO SIT A LABOUR EXAMINATION UNDER CONDITIONS LAID DOWN IN THE EDUCATION ACT. BOYS WHO PASS CAN LEAVE SCHOOL ON THEIR 13TH BIRTHDAY AND COMMENCE FULL – TIME EMPLOYMENT.

Our joy at this announcement was tempered by a few pessimists who cried, 'We shall never pass; they will make it too hard for us.' Did we but know, this was an insidious piece of legislation, the effect of which would plague us for the rest of our lives.

Ma gave her consent, somewhat grudgingly, underlined when she remarked, 'I suppose it's your life, you make your own decision.' Came the Saturday when we were to sit the exam at Waller Street School, 9 a.m. prompt, armed with pen, ink, pencil, rubber and writing paper. The utensils knocked Ma back sixpence. The state could not afford to supply these essentials.

A tall official in a cut-away collar, conveniently making room for his large Adam's apple, shuffled us six feet apart, cleared his throat and proceeded to lay down the rules. 'There are twelve questions on your card, answer any ten. You have four hours, no more, no less, to finish your examination. You may visit the toilet in your own time, no two boys at the same time. Any boy caught cheating, or whispering to the next boy, will be disqualified. Now the clock on the wall says 9.30 a.m. This you may time yourself with.'

Impatient to start, apprehensive of the questions, we grabbed at the brown, dog-eared cards, and devoured them with our eyes. Scanning the card and heeding the advice of Bom Bom, our school teacher, to do the easy ones first, I was disgusted to find them all easy. I wondered, 'Have I got the wrong card?' Adam's Apple, we never knew his real name, looked across at me and suggested I got on with it. This was not the time nor place to argue, I was finished in under two hours.

Putting my hand up in school regulation manner, I asked permission to leave. Adam's Apple gave permission and I made for the exit. 'Not that way, stupid,' he shouted, 'the lavatory is over there.' Speechless, I went back to my place, and idled the session through. Thought I, we had been cheated, they wanted us to leave school, consoling myself with the thought that perhaps our school had given us a good education. Seventy five per cent passed, but this was average for all the schools.

When the results were announced six weeks later, the headmaster called each one of us who had passed into his room. 'Darby,' he said, 'it's no use asking you to stay at school, is it? You know it all.' Little did he know how that remark hurt, because a little persuasion at that time would have kept me at school. He made up my mind for me, so I departed, with a chip on my shoulder, to make a living full-time.

My last day at school was no different from all the other days.

Eight years of scholastic endeavour had resulted in passing the Labour Exam, and reaching the ex. seventh standard. The prefix ex. signified I was excused normal lessons to do school chores. I reminded the head that today was my last day of doing the ink wells. He made a pun from the information: 'Ink, well, well,' and retired, chuckling.

22

The Hat Trade

'Time to settle down,' Ma advised, 'what about the hat trade?' The hat trade it was, fifty four hours a week, twopence per hour. Progress indeed, and Saturday afternoon free.

The factory was like a beehive, workers buzzing everywhere: stiffeners, blockers, steamers, polishers, milliners, machinists – where would I fit in? The boss himself showed me around, starting in the basement. Acknowledging the salutation of one old man who had worked forty years for the firm, 'Good Lord,' I said, swanky like, 'and he is still in the cellar.' My indiscretion received the contempt it deserved, and we mounted the stairs to the ground floor level.

On each side of the long corridor stood small offices, labelled Counting House, Managing Director, Manager, Designer, Forelady, etc. I put my foot in it again, suggesting that no work was done on this floor because it was so quiet. On the first floor aproned females sat on low chairs, legs apart, making huge laps wherein all the paraphernalia of hat trimming reposed. Next floor, stiffeners were dipping straw hats into vats of hot liquid gelatine, all men, in rubber aprons and boots, they looked a fearful lot, offensive like the smell from the sticky gelatine.

Still climbing the everlasting stairs, next step was the blocking room. Here men were at work on machines from which steam issued forth, the sound not unlike that from the trains at the railway station. Suspended at the centre, a rubber bag resembling a cow's udder with the teats cut off. Water under pressure was forced into the bag. The gelatine-impregnated hat took on the shape of the aluminium block in the bottom half of the contraption, when both halves met.

Reaching the top floor, boss and boy stopped to get their breath back, before opening the door to a blast of noise which deafened us. Huge electric motors driving leather belts pulley wheels and shafting round at a terrible speed. They in turn moved needles on seventeen-guinea hat-sewing machines up and down faster than the eye could focus.

Fifty women in long rows facing each other, sewed and shaped straw hats into floppy caricatures of the ultimate Paris fashion. Awestruck, I made no comment. 'Attention, girls,' the boss shouted, 'this is the new lad. Let me hear no complaints after today about your dirty workroom. This will be his first job in the mornings.' Women, mostly matrons, stared at me for a while, saw nothing about me to warrant much attention, and got back to work. Now I knew where I fitted in.

As the weeks passed, I realised that everyone was my boss, father and mother in giving advice and vying with each other in little kindnesses. Having wit, if nothing else, I took full advantage of adult weaknesses and prospered. On Saturday morning, cap out-stretched, I stood at the bottom of the stairs and thanked them politely for coppers they dropped into the hat. Some gave for services rendered, others not wanting to appear mean. Perks from the men mounted up. They mostly drank about four pints of ale daily. This was one of my chores, fetching the booze. In return I kept the money on the returned empties. Every morning I purchased hot pies and rolls from the bakery for the staff. This was an exercise in £.s.d., writing down requirements, price and change for myself. Not having a stomach for all the perks, I pocketed the money instead, but thanked them all the same.

Apart from these pleasantries there was plenty of work to be done. Late afternoon in the basement was one mad rush, making wood frames to protect the frail hat boxes. All must be ready for the railway dray at 4 p.m., if not, I had to load the hat barrow about ten feet high and lug it to Midland Station. On some of these jaunts I thought of Mr. Clarke the butcher, reliving some of those times. Was I right in leaving him? The jingling coppers in my pocket echoed the answer.

The one blot on my career was the half-day visit to the boss's home. His wife smoked, called me by my surname, and nothing satisfied her. Chopping wood for the week, sieving dust from the coal, weeding the garden; all had to be done in one afternoon. She kept me going until 6 p.m. and then it took me half an hour to walk home. I relented somewhat at Christmas after she gave me half a crown and a bag of sweets. As Ma said, even I could be bought.

Knowledge of hats and appreciation of fine workmanship grew with daily handling and packing. Fine Italian pedal straw and glossy Austrian velours were despatched to the best fashion houses of London and Paris, yet this same quality graced the heads of those who made them. Pride would not decree otherwise.

My first awareness of women, other than mothers, came with the starting of a new girl apprentice. She was fourteen, fair haired, done in two plaits and freckled. Trying to break the ice, I offered her an iced bun from my morning collection. She looked at the bun, and with an impolite refusal suggested it was not worthwhile eating after I had mauled it. I took a bite out of it myself and told her she had lost the opportunity of tasting good grub. The frigid little madam hurried away, her buttoned boots echoing down the stone corridor.

'Stuck-up cow,' I shouted after her, and later I stood before the boss to explain, if I could, my misbehaviour.

'Miss Skinner has complained to me about your bad language.'

I explained that having been a butcher, cows came naturally

to me. He left the office, returned with the forelady, and made me repeat what I had previously told him. Scared stiff, I did just that, whereupon they both roared with laughter. Finally straightening his face, the boss warned me not to use that word again to ladies, and let me go.

I met Miss Skinner the next day in the same corridor. 'Is the boss sacking you? Did he tell you off?' she queried.

'No, he is not. If anyone is sacked, it will be you for reporting me,' I countered. Then both of us giggled and the ice was broken. We exchanged Christian names, so Gladys and Aubrey were friends. Clandestine meetings behind piles of hat boxes were arranged, with intimate questions being asked. She asked me if I had loved anyone else, and my reply, 'Only my mother and Clarke's pony,' pleased her. I challenged her with having dozens of blokes; her forceful, 'What do you take me for?' reassured me.

In a rash moment I asked her to come with me to the pictures. Accepting my offer, time and place were arranged. The rest of the day seemed to last for ever in my anxiety to be home and tell Ma. She listened to my description of the young lady, painting in my imagination a word picture so colourful, that Ma, in her whimsical way, asked me if her name was Cleopatra. Then, bringing me back to earth, she reminded me that the only clobber I had was what I stood up in.

'I told you not to wear your suit for work,' she said.

'I can't let her down now,' I wailed. So, forking out a couple of shillings, we went to see what old Lynn, the secondhand man had got. Sorting over the heaps of clobber we came up with a jacket, near enough matching, and Ma set to sponging and pressing the suit. The fit was passable, but in spite of Ma's work they still smelt pawnshoppy.

'Have you any scent, Mum, to take the smell away/'

'Be off boy, and don't get too close to her!' advised Ma, and in the excitement to be off I had no tea.

While waiting outside the pictures for Gladys, three of my pals came along. 'Coming in then?' they asked.

'Soon,' I replied and sauntered away.

The urge to forget the date and rush in after my mates was overwhelming, when a voice behind me said, 'Sorry to keep you waiting.'

Walking up to the pay box I asked for two sixpennies and guided Gladys into the gloom. Tinribs, the old enemy, took the tickets, shone his torch into my face and enquired if I had come into money. Maintaining dignity suitable for this occasion, I trod on his foot and let it go at that.

The film, featuring Harry Houdini, was a thriller. The tense scene, where the hero was suspended over a vat of acid and bound with barbed wire, was so exciting that I scoffed all the liquorice allsorts bought with Gladys in mind. When she asked for one, I could only offer the empty bag. Gladys became silent after this, so I offered to purchase some chips on the way home. 'Keep your old chips,' she retorted, which much relieved me. My remaining cash would not be sufficient for chips and tram fare home. A Fatty Arbuckle comedy soon had her laughing again, and at the end of the show, feeling happy also, I stood to attention while Blue Nose the pianist punched out the King, instead of beating him to it by making my exit.

Gladys lived in High Town, so hurrying past the fish shop, we boarded a tram. The constant swaying of the juggernaut brought us closer together. When she held on to me I felt new awareness of the female sex. Gladys asked me to say goodnight to her before we reached her street, because she had not told her mother we were going out to the pictures. 'You tell her next time,' I advised. 'I told my mother and she didn't mind.' With that she scampered off with a shrill, 'See you tomorrow.'

Pictures now and then, and occasional walks over the hills saw us progress into kissing goodnight. When it rained we would sit in People's Park, huddled together under her umbrella, and plan for the future. One Sunday she asked me home to tea. Ma cautioned me, 'Once you get your feet under the table of a girl's home, you're hooked,' she said, and my, 'Give us a chance, Ma, I'm only fourteen,' failed to alter her deadpan expression.

Remembering the boy's birthday party, I set off cautious and apprehensive, in no mood to be humiliated. I knocked on the door of a small terraced cottage and waited. A carbon copy of Gladys answered the door, presumably her younger sister, and invited me in. One step down, straight into the parlour from the road. Gladys was not in the room, so I introduced myself first to the mother, a pleasant woman who always seemed to be chattering, and then to the father who was eyeing me from over the top of his newspaper. The younger sister shouted up the stairs for Gladys, who entered the room in pink frock and big bowed pigtails.

'Have you been introduced?' she asked.

'Of course he has,' said little sister. 'You should have let him in instead of running upstairs.'

Inane chatter and niceties lasted until tea, the father feigning sleep, saying nothing. Tea was already laid in the back room and I sat between Gladys and her sister. Her mother, chatting away, suggested we start tea without father, and poured the tea in bone china cups, better than my coronation mug! The food was very good: celery, brown and white bread, cakes and pastries.

Halfway through the meal Dad walked in, clutching a bag of winkles. Gladys coloured up and suggested to her father that he eat the winkles some other time. Ignoring her, he shovelled a load of them on my plate, commanded the mother to find me a hatpin, and asked if I liked them.

'Not 'arf!' I remarked.

'Good boy,' he replied, 'Get stuck in!'

I really liked winkles, Ma and I often having them at home. Conversation was now restricted to the winkle eaters, the females giving sidelong glances at our performance, but remaining aloof.

Finally they left the table and we relaxed, discussing everything and nothing.

The finale, when all adjourned to the parlour, was very distressing. The father dozed off and I could make no conversation with three females, who for no apparent reason had lost their tongues. Eventually, the mother said to Gladys, 'I think the young man should be going now.' Gladys fell over her feet in her haste to see me off and made no response to my apology.

Outside all hell let loose. She called me every name under the sun, stupid, dragged-up, ill mannered - all because I had eaten father's winkles.

'You are no different from all the louts I know,' she said.

'How do you know?' I asked.

'Because I've been out with them!'

This really got me going. Calling her a whore and other obscenities, I ran off. For all my resolve, this pretty girl in temper had humiliated me, comparing me with the other louts. Reaching the railway footbridge, I slowed down for want of breath, realised that this was the end to a pleasant interlude, and convinced in my own mind that no other girl would worry me again.

'But what about Ma?' I thought.

The solution? I would tell her nothing.

23

The Crusaders

The honeymoon with Gladys was over. 'Plenty more fish in the sea,' said Ma. I was minded to tell her that in this instance it was winkles.

Back with my pals and the football season to come, it was decided we should start a football team. Having progressed from tincans, ragballs and pigs' bladders into a genuine football case, minus bladder, we had become nifty of foot because of constant practice with the eccentric objects. So we looked around for financial backing, deciding to call our team The Crusaders. Percy Punter, a colleague of mine in the hat trade, owning his own small factory, was selected as the victim. We visited him and outlined our plan, everyone putting a spoke in until Percy, completely nonplussed, advised calling a general meeting and he would try to attend.

Our usual meeting place was the steps leading to Mrs. Buckingham's front door, well-sheltered from the wind, and she, being deaf, could never hear us. For this occasion with Percy present, it had to be done properly. After surveying likely halls, we decided on the Stuart Commercial Café, a working man's char-and-wad dump. For the price of a cup of stewed tea, we could sit there for hours.

So we raided Percy's premises again, in force, and told him we had booked a meeting place, and asked him to be there at 7:30

pm. the following evening. Much to our surprise Percy turned up, so we all trooped in, pushed a couple of tables together and commandeered most of the chairs. The proprietor shuffled over, plucking up courage to chuck us out, but was left speechless when we ordered fourteen cups of tea. Told that our president, Mr. Punter would pay, he strode away, working out how much profit he would make on fourteen cups of tea at a penny a go.

Mr. Punter listened to our suggestions, but when asked for five pounds to buy shirts, socks and football, he got up to go, remarking, 'I cannot possibly raise that amount of ready cash.' The honour of being made our president carried no weight, stage whispers of stinginess hardened him still more. Then a bright lad, who later went into business on his own, came up with a brilliant idea. If Mr. Punter paid for two dozen subscription cards to be printed, bearing his name as president, inviting tradesmen etc. to donate money to the Crusader Football club, we would canvas the town and pay back the five pounds Percy was lending us.

Forgetting Mr. Punter, we crowded round the lad, congratulating him on a wonderful solution. Percy, rather intimidated by it all, agreed to fork out, warning of dire penalty if we defaulted. The same boy who had promoted the deal asked Mr. Punter if he felt hungry, and before he could answer, we all said we're starving. Percy coughed up again with a round of dripping toast.

On the Saturday we purchased a dozen shirts, knicks, a dozen pairs of socks and a football, eking out the fiver with the cheapest we could obtain. Back to the porch, and the election of officers. Monty was made captain, he could kick with both feet. Reg Barnett was made treasurer, he handled money on his uncle's whelk stall. I was made secretary on account of school compositions. The rest were committee members, no one being left out.

The subscription cards arrived, territory for exploitation was parcelled out, but after three weeks our total income was fourteen shillings. Close scrutiny of the cards in daylight revealed rubbing out, alterations, and in one card, no inside pages. The excuse of this boy - his father had torn it out to light his pipe. The fiddling had to stop, so, in full committee, it was decided for each five bob collected, any boy could legally take one shilling for himself. The incentive worked; a fortnight later we had the five pounds.

Summoning Percy to an 'extraordinary' meeting at the café, we paid him back his five pounds. Full of emotion for our honesty, Mr. Punter squandered ten bob on tea and bacon sandwiches all round, made a speech, drank to the future of the club in stewed tea, and went on his way with tears in his eyes, a very happy man.

Resplendent in striped shirts of claret and amber, shortened to red and yeller, we turned out for our first match against Pinky Day's team, the Silver Stars. The game was played on Pope's Meadow, interrupted at times by twenty dogs chasing a bitch. We beat them 19 – 1, their goal coming from Pinky himself, who toe-ended the ball in from the halfway line, our goalie at the time chasing a young supporter of our opponents who had pelted him. We looked good as we left the field, but something would have to be done about our boots. Wellingtons, plimsolls and clogs were not becoming for a team of our potential.

The next game was against a village side, four miles away. Having been given a pair of real football boots, I felt really good for this match. They were on the big side but extra laces held them on. By the time we had walked to the ground it was raining heavily; the pitch, used for grazing cattle, was dotted with cow dung and there was no dressing room accommodation. The village side was much older than ours, and they ran rings around us in the first half, scoring four goals. At half time we had a council of war under the leafless oak tree and decided to rough house them. The rain was still teeming down, soaking the cow dung which we would use to good effect. The tactics were to dribble close to the plentiful pancakes, miskick the ball and kick the dung in the face of the enemy. The plan worked for a time, until the villagers tumbled to it and returned the compliment. We were now getting on top, scoring our fourth and equalising goal. Taking a terrific swipe at the ball, I missed it completely, but my boot sailed through the goal, beating the goalie all ends up. The game ended all square, and in the gathering gloom, soaked to the skin with a four-mile walk back ahead of us, my joke, 'We beat them four goals and a football boot to four!' fell on deaf ears. Cow dung and rain did not mix well with inane remarks.

Hardly any of the teams we played had dressing room accommodation, exceptions being chapel teams, but these religious teams only played each other. Our dressing rooms were under a hedge or the latrine on Dallow Road Rec. and we could not expect them to stoop down to this level. In the spring, with fine weather, we changed at home, walking to the ground in full regalia. We washed our own kit, the once brilliant red and 'yeller' stripes soon fading into pink all over, and shirts in use during the week as vests took on a tacky appearance much deprecated by the more finicky of our team. Still, we won nearly all our matches, were respected by the football fraternity. Our keenest supporter, Percy, the president, philanthropist, referee, linesman and trainer, never regretted being tangled up with our mob, showing his appreciation by inviting us home to tea at the end of the football season.

24

The Diamond

I enjoyed working at the hat factory but realised that my status of errand boy would remain static for some time. Not that I was ambitious, but Ma with her scrimping and scraping irritated me, a few bob more in the kitty would work wonders. So I gave in my notice and found a job at the Diamond Foundry. On the Friday of my departure, Mr. Gee, the hat man, gave me extra pay and wished me well. The women had a whip round and bought me a present, and Gladys, of my short-lived courtship, kissed me goodbye. Full up from such kindness, I nearly asked for my job back.

The following Monday I set out for the Diamond, half an hour's walk from home. I was advised to wear old clothes, which presented no difficulty. My first rebuff was from the gateman, 'Two minutes late tomorrow morning, and you don't come in,' a salutation panicking me into calling him 'Sir' for the first and last time.

Not knowing where to go, I wandered into the casting section, a vast area lit up by shirtless men busy pouring molten iron into squares and oblongs of black sand. The inferno frightened me, so I wandered into a gangway. Then shouts and curses heralded the approach of a man with a jacket on, who pulled me clear of a cauldron of metal descending on me like an express train. A torrent of foul language in a Scotch accent made me aware that he must be the foreman. But when he cast doubts about my birth I saw red and asked him who he thought he was mouthing at.

Momentarily speechless by my query, he gave me time to explain.

'I have to see Mr. Jim Murphy.'

'New boy, eh?' he replied and forthwith hustled me out and directed me to the place where I would be working. Jimmy Murphy, despite his name, was a Scotsman from Falkirk, he said, a kindly man who would persist in spitting chewing tobacco through a gap in his front teeth.

'Laddie,' he said, 'Ye dinna look the part; whatever made ye come here to work?'

'It's the money,' I answered.

'If ye had said ye like the job, I wouldna started ye – hang your jacket on the wall and follow me.'

It was customary in foundries for new boys to be made 'free members', the ritual consisting of removing his trousers and painting his privates with liquid black lead.

The majority of the employees were of Scottish descent, The Diamond having transferred from Falkirk to Luton in 1906. Nearly all chewed tobacco, smoking forbidden, why I never knew, because fire hazards were all over the shop. Being tempted to take a bite of this twist tobacco, black as Newgate's Knocker, I started to chew and was nearly strangled by the revolting weed. I never touched the stuff again. Legend had it that one old codger, expert in expectoration, could drown a blow fly from six feet range.

Working conditions were primitive. The lavatories, called 'bogs', were exposed troughs of concrete along which gravity fed rainwater flushed at frequent intervals. The bare posteriors of users were inevitably splashed by the torrent, a six-inch diameter pole, on which the victim perched, adding to the discomfort. No one lingered. In winter we feared frostbite, in summer, flies; for all seasons, acute pins and needles.

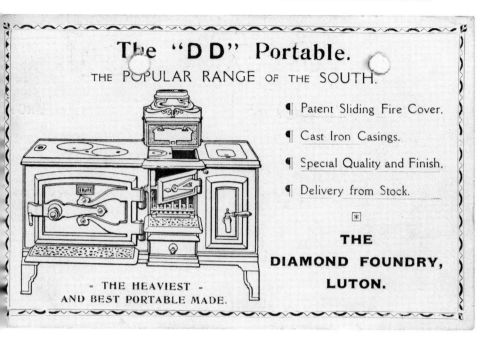

Diamond Foundry receipt card

Rows were settled after work on The Linces, a grassy slope beyond the work's gate. A ring was formed, the two antagonists stripped down to the waist and fought with bare fists. Urged on by a partisan crowd, they bashed away at each other like the old time prize fighters, until one of them collapsed from exhaustion. I had witnessed scrapping in the alley, but this was caveman brutality. They called it fighting in the 'correct manner'. Thus, if two men were seen arguing on the shop floor, the bully boys made certain of entertainment that evening. Refusal to settle outside was, in the long run, worse than going through with it.

There was no canteen, so all workers owned billycans for brewing up tea. Food was brought to work in small wicker baskets, and suspended in the air to avoid the rats. Ma packed me up beef clangers which I heated up on hot castings. This toughened the skin to a degree that peeling was necessary to get at the succulent interior. In summer we ate our dinner on The Linces, in winter, round coke braziers, the central heating of those days.

After dinner the younger boys explored the works. Our favourite haunt was the 'Dock', a goods siding inside the works. Climbing in and out of the wagons, we found much treasure on the wagon floor. One boy found a horseshoe, so we carried out the ritual of spitting on it in turn for luck. Then the finder hurled it from sight. To make certain of good luck we must not see where it fell. The shoe went from sight all right, over the top of a covered wagon. An oath and an irate Mr. Blackwell, General Manager, emerged, carrying the horseshoe and a dented hat.

'Who threw this?' he raved, but no one answered. 'Right, if the culprit does not own up I'll sack the lot of you!'

Then Harry spoke up. 'I didn't throw it at you, sir. I threw it for luck.'

'Name and shop foreman, boy? You're sacked!' he said, 'and if I catch any of you on this dock again you will follow him!'

Returning to the shop and hoping Blackwell's dog died, we came up with an idea to get Harry his job back: the whole shop would strike. But when we canvassed the grownups for support we only got cuffed for our efforts.

Dust extraction was a joke. All our underclothing, including shirts, were 'ironmoulded'. Shirt armpits and the crutch of long pants hanging on clothes' lines, bore testimony to its inadequacies. Silica dust from grinding wheels was made worse by sulphur fumes, so bronchitis was an occupational hazard. I caught the complaint and was away from work for six weeks. A letter from the firm, warning that my job would not stay open indefinitely, made me hasten back to work. Three months later I was ill again and reluctantly forced to leave.

25

The Christadelphian

Near home was a brush shop, proudly proclaiming, 'You name it; we have it'. A pastime of mine in these idle days was to identify the various kinds of brushes and imagine what they were used for. On this particular January morning, looking in the window away from the wind, I saw a man stick a notice on the inside of the glass: *Boy wanted, apply within*. Quickly I patted down my unruly hair, buttoned up my jacket and opened the door. In a posh voice I suggested to the man that I would like the job in the window.

'Would you now?' he answered.

'Yes,' I said and then added a belated 'please.'

He explained that there were other applicants to see, but he would take my address and let me know.

'There aren't any more; I watched you put the notice up,' I countered. This fish was not getting off the hook for any fault of mine. Then a customer walked in and asked for a cheap scrubbing brush. After talking the woman into buying a dear one with a 'lifetime's wear' he returned to me, and my query, 'What's a lifetime's wear, sir?'

'Ha, a lifetime's wear is non-committal, my boy. Now, if I had said the brush would last a lifetime, that would be dishonest. Do you understand?'

'Oh yes, that is very clever, sir.' But I didn't know what he was gabbling on about. To get this job I would have called him, 'Your Majesty.' After some skirmishing he decided to set me on. Twelve shillings a week, for fifty-four hours. Roughly twopence ha'penny an hour.

The first two days were occupied in sticking leaflets, advertising a forthcoming sale, in letter boxes. *All prices slashed, Sacrifice, Can never be repeated*, stated the leaflets. They impressed me, if not the public. I felt sorrow for him. My instructions were to deliver the leaflets in residential areas, but to me, the mean terraced slums in my area were residential. Why should they not have the chance at giveaway prices? Besides, having no long garden paths to walk along made distribution less tiring. Having completed this first task, my next job was to clean out the areas under the gratings which people walked over. This job was awful, because when I looked above my head I could see the bloomers and thighs of women gazing in the brush shop window. I complained to the boss, but all I got from him was, 'They are potential customers, work quietly and don't disturb them.'

The job was not hard, compensation for the low wages maybe, and I settled down. The boss seemed satisfied and taught me how to serve the customers. Then on Wednesday, half-day, he asked me home to tea. I clashed with religion again. He told me all about his beliefs as a Christadelphian, suggesting that I attend his next gospel meeting.

'Do you go to any church?' he asked, and the negative answer pleased him.

'Good, you can start with us.'

I escaped further inquisition by promising to attend his Bible lecture on the following Sunday evening, and hurried home, my half day wrecked and religion to come on Sunday night.

'Go along boy, there's no harm in it; perhaps you will finish up with tea and cake.'

There was no escape. After the shop closed at 9 p.m. on the

following Saturday, the boss's wife came in, informed me that I would have tea with them on Sunday, then we should go to the lecture in the evening together.

The lecture, given by my boss to an audience of nine, was *The Interpretation of the Book of Revelations*. I listened intently. If the lecture was to be debunked I had got to know what he said. Besides I wanted to keep the job, but no religion with it. After a brief prayer in which the blessing was asked for new converts, the meeting broke up with handshakes all round.

Monday, morning, with an extra warm, 'Good morning, friend,' from the boss, and I waited for the inevitable, 'Tell me what impressed you most last night?'

'Nothing, I have heard it all before,' I replied.

Taken aback he reminded me that I had not been a churchgoer. Then he told me only Christadelphians would enter the Kingdom of Heaven, surely that was what I desired.

'You will be telling me next that the world will be coming to an end shortly,' I countered.

Sure enough, the old patter came. 'There is definite proof in the Book of Revelation that the end is near,' he warned me.

Then I played my ace. 'Why don't you go about in sackcloth and ashes, like old Mene did a few years ago, if you are so sure of the end?'

White with annoyance at my unco-operative manner, he queried, 'Who in God's name is old Mene?'

It was the opening I wanted, so I told him about how Mene had prophesied, how he had set the time and date, how he had sold a flourishing business, donned sackcloth, and gone around the streets carrying a banner, frightening gullible people out of their lives, of the September night of the full moon, when hundreds of people gathered on the hills and waited for the end. How, when nothing happened, they pelted him with cow dung and clods of earth, and how he regained respectability and started up in business again.

I told him of Brother Duck, who exploited cripples and halfwits. The new Messiah he called himself, and charged twelve miserable wretches two shillings weekly for being his disciples.

A customer came in and stopped the cackle and during that week nothing else was mentioned about religion.

The atmosphere was somewhat tense during this period, and occasionally, when I looked up, he would be gazing at me. A week later his wife asked me to tea on my half day, saying that it would be company for her, the boss having business in London. The tea was excellent; having once told her that I liked winkles they were on the table.

After tea she played the piano for a while, then sat beside me and began to talk. 'It would make my husband happy,' she said, calling me Aubrey, 'if you tried to understand him. Why don't you join the Christadelphians and become one of us? There is so much in life you are missing.'

By this time I really felt uncomfortable. I wanted to go to the toilet and dare not ask; she was too close to me. I was perspiring, and both religion and the woman had me confused. Looking at my wrist, where there was no watch, I stammered, 'It's getting late,' moved to the door and hurriedly departed, forgetting to say goodnight.

On my next half day the boss asked me to call in and be introduced to a great friend of his. 'Just call in about 3 p.m., we won't keep you long.'

Again I fell into the trap. For two hours this great friend, an authority on biblical matters, spoke of Heaven, Hell, the Awful Judgement to come, until I thought, 'This man knows so much, he must be the Almighty in disguise.' Still I would not give way, and I went home distressed to tell Ma about it.

'I don't suppose the Good Lord has made his own mind up yet,' she philosophised, 'so how can mere mortals know?'

The final encounter came after weeks of pettiness when I

could do nothing right. He started up once more on religion, hinting that he would like an assistant who was a member of his Gospel Mission. Stung by this backhander, I discarded the little refinements acquired from serving customers, telling him to stick his job and the Christadelphians where the monkey stuffed his nuts. It was the end. Who was at fault? Shrugging it off, I said, 'Who cares?'

During the war I went back to butchering temporarily, the butcher having lost his slaughterman to a greater slaughter. All else taking a back seat to the beckoning blue smock and striped apron at the door, with beef to be killed on Monday, mutton on Tuesday and pork on Wednesday, there was little time left for idling.

Old man and boy, a fifteen hundredweight Hereford looking balefully over the pen door, thirty feet of hemp rope, pole axe and stubbed post to pull the beast on to, set the stage.

'Sling the rope over the Hereford, play the other end out, and slip it through the post hole, hold the rope taut. If he runs, you run, pulling the rope as you run. Have you got it?'

A subdued 'Yes.'

The old man opens the pen door and the beast lumbers out, guided towards the tethering post by the prodding butcher. Scared boy secures the rope and breathes normally again. Before dispatching the noble animal, the butcher, long out of practice with the pole axe, pauses and takes a piece of snuff. The animal, head tied down, becomes restless.

'Go on, Sir,' I whisper, 'kill him before he breaks loose.' I didn't relish having to lasso a maddened animal. A few practice swipes, then he advanced on the Hereford. He swung. I closed my eyes. Thud: the beast was down.

'We've done it, boy!' he shouted, and snuffed it again in celebration. I also would be in at the death.

The greater slaughter was rising to a crescendo. No abode, mansion or hovel, was spared its dead. Paper boys came into their own as excitement of so-called victories stirred the populace. I was tempted to go back into papers, but loyalty to the butcher prevailed. Instead, I asked for more money and got an extra shilling a week rise.

The town was filling up with soldiers, Leicesters, Lincolns, Notts and Derbys, Artillery; the whole British Army seemed to be with us; 'the goings-on' as Ma called them, 'shocking'. Troops were compulsorily billeted on everyone, wagging tongues making full use of the situation. Pregnant women were asked when last their husbands were home, the war secondary to the moralisers and scandalmongers.

Four soldiers were billeted on us at a shilling nightly for each one, no bedding provided. Cups of tea at a penny, added to our income. We were further enriched by food our guests pinched from the cookhouse. This extra supply dried up when a snap inspection by the quartermaster unearthed a fifty-six pound cheese in the cellar. Ma got away with it, the troops got 'jankers'. When the soldiers left, our prosperity went with them, so we were to know poverty again.

Left over was the remount depot, a few hundred men in army huts, who stayed for the duration of the war. Food became scarce, ground maize being used as a substitute for flour. This diet overheated the blood, an epidemic of boils resulting. An issue of black treacle, little better than molasses used in foundries for corebinding, was a gastronomic nightmare; so was cocoa butter with its rancid taste.

Gossip no longer pointed the finger, young girls being encouraged to visit the remount depot. Tins of jam and margarine were rich reward for loan of the body. Ma got to know that Tommy Liptons and the Maypole would be selling margarine on the same day, so she queued at Liptons, and I went to the Maypole. We queued nearly all day. Ma got half a pound, I got none. They wouldn't serve children.

Influenza took its toll. Coffin makers were hard put to satisfy demand. The government was forced to issue ration cards, but the mounting toll of influenza and consumption was beginning to match strides with the slaughter in Flanders.

The war came closer with the appearance of Zeppelins, special constables with hand bells warning people when the cigar-shaped monsters were overhead. All lights had to go out, the throbbing engines of the intruder adding to the confusion. Crowds of boys running on to the hills, hoping for a sight of a Zeppelin, were rewarded one night when Lieutenant Robinson destroyed one. From a distance of sixteen miles we cheered the falling monster, our faces lit up by the enveloping flames.

The Jutland battle, hailed as a victory in the Nelson style, left us cold. Twenty-one ships sunk, and thousands of sailors drowned, was a price even the most patriotic found difficult to stomach. Apart from sudden bursts of excitement, the war began to create instability at home. Wives of men overseas resented women with husbands in this country. One woman pinned a white feather on a soldier in civilian clothes. The soldier, home on leave from France, promptly knocked her down. In the riot that followed, many people were injured. Another man came home on leave, listened to gossip, and cut his wife's throat.

Females were becoming more masculine in appearance, driving coal carts and trams; there were even lady dustmen. Where the male sex were concerned women became the hunters.

Mons. The Marne. Ypres. The Argonne, names everyone became familiar with, but with Ma's failing eyesight I was to become familiar with London. On my ride to London in the train, with nose pressed to the carriage window, I watched the countryside slip by, vast new pastures I would explore one day. St. Pancras, a cathedral of glass and iron, sheltering giant steam engines panting off. Outside, trams without tramlines and a bewildering sea of traffic. The tube, an underworld of slamming doors, echoes and toy trains speeding like the wind. People scurrying like leaves in an autumn storm, and the lifts moving up and down defying forces of gravity. London, the heart of the Empire! I saw it all, yet saw nothing. I had to get to Moorfields; the job came first.

The London visits over, the tube, St. Pancras, a little of the city, I could discourse on these, but when my pals asked about the Thames, The Tower and Trafalgar Square, my imagination had to suffice. They had never been to London, so when I told them Nelson's Monument was as high as the clouds, none disputed my tall story.

Back to earth, the war dragged on, highlighted by the sinking of the Lusitania. I remembered the Titanic going down and the singing of 'the band was playing as the ship went down'. The background to that tragedy was peace, but with the Lusitania, propagandists saw the possibilities of bringing the Americans into the conflict. Righteous indignation saw certain victory with America on our side. Still the war would drag on before America came in and a million more men had yet to die.

26

The Workhouse

December 1918. The war was over, munitions were no longer a matter of life and death. So the old men, women and boys were stood down. Monday and Thursdays I waited outside the local newspaper offices, grabbed the paper still wet with print, and scanned the jobs vacant column. If a job was going, a mad dash to the place, only to find a crowd of job seekers there already. I was no slouch when it came to running, but this lot must have sprouted wings. The scarcity of work was aggravated by returning soldiers demanding priority in the work stakes.

Mother's eyes were failing at this time, so reluctantly we asked Mr. Powers, the Relieving Officer, for help. His office was conveniently situated in the back entrance to the Workhouse, away from gossips who would then spread news of our having to seek charity. Being a nice gentleman, he listened to our story, ascertained we were in need, and gave us a voucher for groceries. The list barred so-called luxuries such as butter, biscuits, bacon. Forbidden also, all but the cheapest cuts of meat – total expenditure not to exceed four shillings in any week. However, we did gorge on hot suet pudding with treacle, and neck of mutton stew. Ma, peering at me across the table, assured me that having had enough to eat was the same as having a banquet.

Compared with some of our contemporaries, life was tolerable. Empty houses were there in plenty, but in the interests of economy parents reared families, the children in turn grew up and had children, all in the same abode. Soon the grandparents became a liability, resigned to going into the Workhouse. There were almshouses, reserved for widows of the middle class, which seemed odd, for these widows usually had money in their own right. Though the Workhouse had a good intake, it never became full up. The old people didn't last long once inside, not so much heart failure as broken heart.

Old age was dreaded, the pension of five shillings weekly inadequate. Even so, quite a number failed to qualify for this meagre sum. The pension was confiscated on entry, to pay for board and lodging, a generous Poor Law doling out a bag of boiled sweets to the females, an ounce of bacca to the males every Saturday evening with no strings attached. Able-bodied males chopped firewood and hawked it round the town on hand carts: even old Clarke's pony would have shied at these loads. The fit females did laundry work, so none became bored with inactivity. Ma and I often visited old friends in the Workhouses, the smell of soup and old age wafting strong as we traipsed along the stone-flagged corridors. The inmates wore uniform, men in grey jackets and trousers in a heavy homespun material, the women in long grey frocks, a colour scheme blending perfectly with the environment. After our visit, Mother would cry on the way home, then lose her temper and rant on, so much that I felt it was my fault these things happened.

At Christmas, society made amends, serving up roast beef, plum pudding and mince pies. Good ladies, clerics, mayor and corporation outdoing each other for the good cause. Beer was also on the menu, though the men of temperance had forebodings about strong drink. Small money gifts were most welcome, for these old people had halfpenny insurance burial policies. Were they to lapse, the Parish would bury them, a last indignity too awful to contemplate. We were not allowed to see our friends on Christmas Day, but on Boxing Day we visited them, doing our best to prolong the spirit of the Joyful Day.

Ma always came away from the Christmas visit in good humour.

'Do you know, boy?' she said, 'I would give my back teeth to hear one of the paupers get up and recite *Christmas Day in the Workhouse*. Then she paused, 'Mind you, after he had scoffed his pudding!'

There were no complaints of ill-treatment in the Workhouse. They were fed, clothed and housed; but the greyness and lack of imagination for the needs of aged people, cast off by their own flesh and blood, led to an indifference which was intolerable. No less appalling was the inhumanity shown by the children of these unfortunate people. This was the twentieth century, and still the shadow of Dickens haunted these institutions.

27

Peace

Peace hath her victories: flag waving and jollification endorsed these noble sentiments, but the reckoning was yet to come. Plans for a memorial were mooted, wise men arguing long, before deciding on the obelisk, surmounted by a figure resembling the Angel Gabriel. All four sides of the memorial would be disfigured with the names of the town dead, in alphabetical order. Thus, the bereaved could more easily identify their loved ones, in spite of the small print. The host of names was a shocking indictment against war, yet the far-sighted planners left space available on the lower plinth for the certainty of war a generation later.

Screaming headlines of allied victories, the telegram boy with his message of death, they were no more. Without stimulation and uncertainty, peace became a bore, grief for the fallen turning into dry-eyed resentment against the established order. Demobilisation was a shambles, the women complaining most who had been starved so long of marital bliss. Especially sore were those whose husbands, despite being first in, were last to come home.

The Government issued civilian suits to the demobbed, but though there was a choice of colour, like Ike and Mike they all looked alike. Some were given trilbies, those with big ears having an advantage, others resembled pimples on gateposts.

Nothing was spared for the welfare of the heroes. Lloyd George, carried away by his own eloquence, promised an acre and a cow for one and all, some taking this too literally, others complaining that all they got was the cow.

Cash grants to tide over the switch were doled out, but still they grumbled, a naïve administration wailing from the mountain top, 'What more do they want?' When the dole ran out, ex-service men occupied the idle hours by serenading us with music. Groups of men, with instruments various, bashed out patriotic songs, whilst the treasurer, begging bowl alert, squeezed coppers from reluctant pedestrians.

A shameful sight watching these cast-offs shuffle along the gutter in Indian file, and there was no escape, they operated on both sides of the street. One veteran, probably left over from the Boer War, exploited the situation by banging on a big drum, a solo effort, unmusical but most effective. Much was said of a land fit for heroes, but little was being done. The town was supposed to be liberal, but like the poor and aged of pre-war days, the qualities of liberalism seemed not to apply.

Plans for a Peace Day celebration went ahead, a great banquet in the Town Hall, the civic heads being given priority. We would watch a procession of the gormandisers enter the Banqueting Hall. No plans for a memorial service were made. Presumably, the Deity, having granted peace, could be dispensed with. Protests failed to move the city fathers, who loaned Wardown Park, the site chosen by the demobbed for a drum-head service, to an Amusement Fair. Belatedly the moor was offered, but this dog-fouled substitute was angrily rejected.

The Mayor was blamed for everything, so on Peace Day the mob invaded the Town Hall, the civic heads preparing for the feast scampering in all directions. The mob, now in full possession, without leadership, for want of what to do next, solved the problem by hurling the furniture out of the windows.

Wind of the riot reached us on Pope's Meadow, where

3pm, 19/7/1919
Town Hall before the 'Peace Riots'

watching set-piece firework displays depicting the King and war
leaders was beginning to bore us. A squib in the hand was worth
more than fireworks seen from a distance, so we dashed off to
the riot and perched on the window ledge of the Free Library.
Above the din jeering crowds could be heard, louder mouths
crying, 'Lynch the Mayor! Burn him out! Hang the bastard!'
We cheered and got goosepimples.

Soon a small fire started in the Town Hall ration-card office,
and gallon cans of petrol, conveniently stored in a garage
opposite, stoked it into a good blaze. The onlookers, seeing a
cheerful fire, suddenly became good-tempered and happy.

Then the police appeared, charging downhill in full force,
truncheons at the ready. This was a gallant attempt but ill-advised,
the crowd being too dense, and unable to scatter, had to stand

3pm, 20/7/1919
Town Hall after the 'Peace Riots'

their ground. The police, meeting up with the immovable force, laid about them with truncheons. The crowd, like cornered rats, suffered grievous injuries, and the police were seen no more. The firemen came next, but quickly retreated, leaving behind damaged engines and chopped-up fire hose.

The Town Hall, now well alight, gave forth a merry spectacle. Ominous creaks from the windows of our vantage point gave an awareness of uncomfortable heat, forcing us to vacate our seats and mingle with the rioters. Someone had read the Riot Act, it was rumoured, but with his hullabaloo he could have been reciting *The Charge of the Light Brigade*. Who cared? No police, no fire brigade, the night was for the enjoying.

The looting of shops surrounding the Town Hall started with the music shop, where a piano was taken from the window and hauled into the road. A pianist of no mean quality thumped out popular songs, to the delight of budding Carusos, who bellowed *Keep the Home Fires Burning* to an accompaniment of 'More, More!' The burning backcloth was to a scene of pilferers matching odd shoes into pairs and doing swaps to accommodate foot size. Umbrella shops, chemists – no properties were sacrosanct, and somehow this carry-on spoiled the jollity.

It was after midnight now, and a sadness hung over the scene of destruction. The dying flames of the Town Hall seemed loath to give up the ghost, occasionally showering sparks, and licking the gutted shell in search of new life.

The clock, which had stood inviolate since the Crimean War, at last gave in, hurtling down with a last defiant note, the flames bursting out once more in sympathy with the death of time. I thought of the clock, the same timepiece had forewarned me with seven gongs every morning that it was time to get out of bed, had comforted me in the small hours, when scared stiff, I lay awake listening to thunderstorms in the August night, had been a watchman crying, 'All's Well!' when the dreaded zeppelins droned overhead. Never again would I hear and see the clock from my attic bedroom window. So I cursed its destroyers and hurried towards home, apprehensive and afraid, with the wrath of my mother to come.

Home at last, I found the door bolted against me, banged loud and was let in. Ma opened up with, 'Where have you been?' as if she didn't know. 'You could have been done in, with all the hooligans on the streets.' Then quietening down, she demanded to know all that had happened, busy all the time, brewing hot chocolate and making dripping toast.

I spoke of the looting, and was made to swear I had nothing to do with that, of the fire and the police charge, but with the clock still worrying, I kept harping on it.

'When Father came home from the Boer War he didn't set fire to buildings,' I reasoned.

Ma, turning away from toasting, snapped back, 'Him? Set light to anything? He was too idle to light the kitchen stove.'

Holding my tongue, I resolved it was useless to ever think of bridging the gulf between Ma and Pa, and suggested we go to bed.

Sunday morning. In the light of day the Town Hall looked a pitiful sight, with the acrid stench of burning wafting everywhere. Young soldiers ringed the Town Hall, with rifles and bayonets. Surely they did not expect anyone to run off with the ruins, but if intimidation was the aim, that had no success, for ribald remarks and banter encouraged the soldiers to join in with wit and good humour.

The appearance of mounted police from London, it was said, annoyed the people, with riff-raff bent on mischief going into huddles with plans for more destruction. A great crowd gathered in Chapel Street with the object of burning down the Corn Exchange. The police, having wind of it, were waiting, and as the mob gathered momentum and raced towards their objective, the well-disciplined force met them head on. Unlike the night before, the crowd checked, then scattered, the police laying about them with great enthusiasm.

Being one of a multitude of boys, enjoying every moment, we knew every alley and bolthole, disappearing and appearing to our hearts' content, the police ignoring us as they pursued bigger game. Eventually, one bobby nabbed me, asked where I lived, cuffed me, and sent me off home.

Numerous arrests were made, but apart from a skirmish at the police station with a view to rescuing the detained rioters, it was all over. There were no winners, only losers, paying extra rate burden for the next decade. Gaol sentences were varied, three years maximum down to three months. Later, it was said that the sentences were lenient, but weighing up what caused this outburst from respectable citizens, the sentences were penal and harsh.

28

The Aftermath

The War Memorial, erected in 1922, became popular as a rendezvous for paper sellers and idlers. Salvationists looked upon it as an intruder, it being bang on the spot where the big drum should be. Wreaths and flowers still adorned the base, but 'sweat' from the 'Copper Angel' streaked down the stonework with cuprous oxide. Lest we not forget the fate of Ames' Pepperbox, some future planner may remove it to some outlandish field.

A new town hall was on the agenda, stopgap or background to the Memorial, posterity must be served. Meanwhile, the welfare of the townsfolk would be forgotten. The Hall was duly built and opened with pomp and ceremony, but three more years would pass before a new hospital worthy of the sick would be paid for by public subscription.

Cheap electricity, low rateable values, and land in abundance were inducements to bring industry into the town, but to the inhabitants of New Town, High Town and Park Street, electric light was unheard of; some had not even gas. Low rates were a belly laugh; justice would appear to be done if these people were paid by the council to live in such hovels. Land in abundance did not apply to the children of Langley Street, Buxton Road and Queen Square Schools, who frolicked on asphalt playgrounds, smaller than a ten pole allotment.

The exaggerated prosperity of the town sucked in workless from all over the country, and local unemployed were aghast at the new invasion. Later historians wrote, 'It was only thirteen per cent of the work force.' Many, like me, who were unemployed at this time, saw it in a different context. To us it meant fewer jobs to go round, and rock bottom wages.

I found work at last, when the Swedish firm Electrolux came into being. The factory was already in existence, having been a French-owned aeroplane factory. Every morning I presented myself at the factory gates, hoping to be called. A fortnight later I was allowed into the interview room. The inquisition, for such it was, by a Mr. Moore, the Works foreman, was successful, and I was set on at eightpence an hour. The rate was a fair one, comparing favourably with district wages. There were plans for an Electrolux village to house the workers, but the idea clashed with local interests and the scheme was forgotten. Compared with the slog and filth of the Diamond foundry, the conditions were excellent. Welding was taught, a trade I exploited through the years, new interests and new friends made life pleasant, and at home, relaxed and more secure. Ma and I were very comfortable.

The Depression of 1929 brought about by the Wall Street Crash seemed, at first, a threat to our happiness, with short-time working and lengthening dole-queues. A means test, coinciding with reduced assistance, heaped more hardship on a struggling community. Men lost what dignity they had, offering to work for less pay than the fortunate men who had jobs.

29

Going Back

It was my lot to be born at the beginning of the twentieth century, to know and accept poverty. Now, in old age, I can chuckle and speak of those times without rancour. All the characters mentioned in my memoirs helped to make my life interesting. Without them life would have been very grey.

Opportunity, of late, has arisen for me to retire away from the town. Already the town's appearance has changed from the scene of my childhood. If I do go away, it will be with an understanding that I can return, before ring roads and bulldozers destroy every haunt of my youth.

I go back, to walk the streets of my childhood, to relieve the ache inside me, the ache which has persisted since I left the town. Perchance I may see some childhood mate, someone who has survived the years. This I must do. The prime characters of those days have long since gone, yet in the shades of eternity they may be peering out. This is not sentiment, it is old age trying to evaluate then and now. The young may say, 'You can't go back,' but they have not the wealth of years. Today I'll go back to my youth, to compare, to find my contemporaries, to judge.

I stand in Princess Street, a royal name for a rough thoroughfare.

'Day dreaming, boy, always day dreaming, and your tea on

the table. Get inside, boy, you'll be late for your paper round.'

And I wake up to see workmen levelling off the rubble of what was once my beloved home.

'What are you levelling off this area for?' I ask.

'To make way for the new Court House,' was the fearful reply. And I shivered at the death of my birthplace.

Higher up the road still stand the two pubs, glaring at each other across the street. *Pretty Woman* and *Star and Garter*, regal still amidst the desolation. The open door of the Star invites me in. Old Hull, the landlord, snatches the empty from my grasp, and bellows, 'You will get no penny on this bottle, you pinched it from the yard!'

A homely barmaid enquires, 'What can I get you, Sir?'

I stammer, 'A pint of bitter please, Madam,' and look around the bar. No spittoons, no scrubbed deal tables, no long benches, no vicious red-haired landlord slopping pints with hairy, shirtless arms, no inane chatter from chokered be-capped scruffs. A beard here and there, but no mandarin moustaches to suck off the frothy ale.

Today, well-dressed customers, caressing whisky glasses, were discoursing in accent varied about yesterday's match on the telly. Ornate bar, shining mirrors, and carpeted floor, emphasised the affluence of the times, but I recognised none of my contemporaries in this sea of nonentities. I was glad, preferring to find them in the back alley, more our environment than the gin palace.

Around the corner in Adelaide Street, what a joy. Here is the butcher's shop, where once I toiled. Shading my eyes to look inside the windowed door, I behold the ice box. No, it's now a fridge. The wind-up telephone is gone for ever. The bowls of wood, which served for tills, usurped by clanking registers, enough to set the teeth on edge. The flies have gone, but the meat still there, frozen still in the embrace of artificial ice.

The proud name of Harry Clarke is no longer ribboned above

the shop, but Moffett - I didn't recall the initial – reads stark in its place. Still, I chuckle as I walk. What misery old Harry Clarke must endure, if there is no snuff in the place where he has gone before.

Into the back alley, known as Stuart Place. Most of the cottages have gone to make way for greasy garages and store dumps, the glittering façade of Wellington Street hiding its rubbish in the alley where once people lived and died. Ike Adams, the poacher, and Sooty Clifton, the sweep, punching each other sober after the pubs chucked out, to our delight and the neighbours' disgust, for they thought the alley was respectable. Today it is the knife and cosh, more sophisticated but less manly.

At the bottom of the alley, the stables of Prince, Harry Clarke's pony, now a boarded-up store. I could not see inside, but guessed at something sinister. I see this beautiful pony, with flaxen mane and tail, the impatient whinny at daybreak when walking down the alley to feed him. He recognised my tread, and I feel for the scars of his playful bite. The beast was my first real love, and I pray that he rides the sky.

Stuart Street, what have they done? Destruction, desecration and desolation; is nothing sacrosanct in furthering the progress of the horseless carriage? Byfield, the Cornman, where I bought a halfpenny worth of locust beans, and chewed on the hard sweet bean for hours; Cox, the Fruit, a pennyworth of specky oranges fed a family with vitamins for a week; the paper shop, where we swopped second-hand blood and thunders, all bulldozed away.

The Duke of Edinburgh and the Bedford Arms, where we found it easier to return the empties, they are no more. The Commercial Hotel, where tea in thick cups and a cheese roll knocked the drayman back a penny-halfpenny for his morning beaver – this haven is no more. Stacey, the Sweet, a benevolent sweetshop proprietor, who dispensed soapy chocolate at cut prices when the sun shone too brightly on his window display. These haunts of my boyhood, disappeared.

In place of all this, roads, described as ring, race tracks in the offing, encouraging pollution, raucous noise and death in the offing. Madmen hunched over the driving wheels, all in a desperate hurry to get nowhere in the quickest possible time. Have they no soul for specky oranges and locust beans? Or will they, suppose they survive sixty years hence, yearn for the motor-car age in the time of mono rail, heliport and moon trip.

Along the awful road is King Street Congregational Church, with the free breakfast of the fish day, the P.S.A. appreciating the singing of local nightingales. But more, the warmth of the interior on winter afternoons with nowhere else to go. I walk up the steps but cannot go in. A notice reads: 'This church is closed. The building is unsafe.' So the nightmare is now become a reality. Fall down majestic spire; there is no place amongst these Philistines. Make way for a stable to harbour the passing juggernauts.

Down the hill to the end of Stuart Street, where Fred Young's glass shop looked across to Brother Duck's Temple. Brother Duck, quack, quack; and away we run, with the new Messiah raving at our heels. Alas, he would have to circumvent a concrete jungle, were he here. A sobering thought: what if we meet up with him in the life to come?

Across Chapel Street, the Great Scar now rearing off the ground, ugliness personified in the souls of its creators.

What have they done to Pikes Close? - beloved of courting couples, and my short cut to the fish shop, where old men, sculptors in their own right, fashioned fantastic shapes from wood. Even Tommy Thorne's bailiff's office gone. Though not in that forgotten past, distressed householders would have sighed with relief not to have Tommy send in the 'Bums'. Could Tommy and his henchmen; Castle Street, home of the Quaker Church and burial ground; Coulson the Fruit; the pawnshop; 'The Dog'; Neville the buryingman, and the inevitable Union Chapel – all disappear?

I search for Dr. Bone's house and surgery, he who quenched the fire in my belly. It's gone to make way for a roundabout, blasphemy of the blessed fairground. No one can tame the mechanical horse, nor will the bulldozer halt its rampaging destruction. The one will strangle with its noxious breath, the other will mangle, no stopping for breath. So be it, my days are numbered; I shall escape the living death.

It's evening now, and I have been back, have seen, compared, judged. Progress for me is in the past. Today is reality; tomorrow, the Lord be praised, I shall not see.